NEP STUDENTS GUIDE FOR UNDERSTANDING NOVEL

A PRACTICAL RESOURCE FOR STUDENTS & TEACHERS

DR. VISHWANATH BITE

Dedicated to

My Grandmother,

Late. Smt. Laxmi Shankar Bite,

Who taught me to be helpful to others

and

Be a Good Human Being before being anything else!

Contents

Introduction

"Have you ever wondered how a simple tale can transport you across time and place, deepening your understanding of the human experience? The novel is not just a collection of words; it's a doorway to new worlds and perspectives. Whether you're a high school or college student trying to make sense of complex themes in literature class, an English teacher aiming to ignite a passion for reading among your students, or a young adult reader looking to enhance your reading experience, this book is for you."

In today's fast-paced world, where distractions abound, the novel offers a unique refuge—a chance to engage deeply with complex characters and themes that reflect our lives. By exploring how novels are constructed, we unlock the potential for richer discussions and insights in the classroom. Understanding the components of novels isn't just for taking a test or completing an assignment; it's about gaining the skills to fully appreciate the transformative power of literature. These skills will allow you to see beyond the surface of a story and connect on a deeper level with its characters and themes.

Think about the last great novel you read. What drew you in? Was it the setting that felt so real you could almost touch it? Or perhaps the characters whose decisions and dilemmas mirrored your life's struggles? Maybe the intricate plot kept you turning pages late into the night. Each element—setting, character, plot, and theme—is a building block of the novel. And just like a house stands more sturdily when each brick is laid with care, your understanding of literature becomes more robust when you grasp how these foundational elements work together.

This book, "Understanding Novel," is designed to guide you through the evolution of the form, dissect its essential elements, investigate various genres, and equip you with the analytical tools to appreciate its depth and complexity. We'll start by looking at how novels have evolved, from the epics of ancient civilisations to the modern-day bestsellers lining bookstore shelves. This historical context will give you a greater appreciation of how the novel has adapted to reflect changing societal values, technological advancements, and shifts in cultural norms.

Next, we'll dive into the essential elements of a compelling novel: the setting, characters, plot, and theme. You'll learn to identify and analyse these components in any novel you read by breaking down them. You'll also gain insight into why certain novels resonate more deeply than others and how authors use these elements to convey their messages effectively.

After we've covered the basics, we'll explore different genres of novels. From mysteries that keep you guessing to romance novels that tug at your heartstrings, each genre has its conventions and unique appeal. Understanding these can enhance your reading experience and give you a broader perspective on what literature offers.

Finally, we'll arm you with the analytical tools to engage with novels critically. Whether you're writing an essay for school or want to discuss a book with friends, having a toolkit of literary analysis techniques will help you articulate your thoughts clearly and persuasively. You'll learn how to identify literary devices, interpret symbolism, and make connections between the text and broader societal issues.

As you turn the pages, consider this your invitation to read and interact with novels. Each chapter serves as a stepping stone, beckoning you to uncover the layers of meaning woven into every narrative. Think of this journey as an exciting exploration where every discovery adds to your understanding and appreciation of literature.

So, grab your favourite book, settle into a comfortable chair, and prepare for this literary adventure. As you delve into the intricacies of novel study, remember that your insights and interpretations are valuable. Literature is a conversation that spans generations and cultures, and your voice adds to its richness. Let's dive in together and unlock the wonders novels offer.

Through this book, you'll find that studying novels is more than an academic exercise—it's an opportunity to connect with stories that mirror our own experiences and those that open windows into lives vastly different from ours. This connection fosters empathy, broadens perspectives, and enriches our understanding of the human condition. You might discover parallels with your life in the challenges faced by a nineteenth-century protagonist or find solace in a contemporary character's triumph over adversity.

Moreover, exploring novels allows you to recognise the craftsmanship behind the storytelling. You'll begin to see how authors weave together plot twists, develop multifaceted characters, and create vivid settings that transport you to different worlds. This newfound awareness enhances your reading enjoyment and sharpens your critical thinking skills, which are invaluable in various aspects of life beyond literature.

For teachers and educators, this book aims to serve as a practical guide to fostering a love of reading and critical analysis among your students. By providing structured approaches and activities, you'll be better equipped to inspire thoughtful discussions and engage students in meaningful exploration of literary texts. Your role in shaping their appreciation for literature is pivotal, and this book strives to support you in that endeavour.

For young readers, whether you're tackling novels for school or personal interest, this book will help you navigate the vast landscape of literature with confidence. You'll learn to approach novels analytically, appreciating the subtleties that make each story unique and discussing your insights with clarity and conviction. Through this journey, you'll become a more discerning reader, able to extract more profound meanings and appreciate the beauty of well-crafted narratives.

In conclusion, "Understanding Novel" is more than just a guide—it's an invitation to immerse yourself in the world of literature, question, analyse, and appreciate the art of storytelling. Whether you're a student, educator, or avid reader, this book provides the tools to deepen your engagement with novels and enrich your reading experience. Let's embark on this journey together, uncovering the layers of meaning in every narrative and discovering the profound impact that great stories can have on our lives.

Novel

Novels are one of the most popular forms of storytelling, offering readers an immersive experience in the characters' lives, the intricacies of plots, and the depths of human emotions. For young adults stepping into the vast world of literature, novels act as a bridge to different cultures, periods, and ways of thinking. In this essay, we'll explore the core elements that make a novel and the various types of novels, illustrated with examples from world literature. By the end, you'll have a clearer understanding of what novels are and how they come to life through words.

What is a Novel?

A novel is a long, fictional story that involves characters, settings, and events intricately woven together to form a narrative. It allows readers to dive deep into a world created by the author, often exploring human emotions, relationships, and ideas in a way that shorter forms like short stories or poems may not. Novels provide an expansive canvas where themes and characters can be developed over hundreds of pages, offering a more in-depth experience.

Think of a novel as a long journey that unfolds slowly, giving you time to immerse yourself in the characters' lives, explore their world, and witness how events affect them.

Elements of a Novel

To fully appreciate a novel, it's essential to understand the key elements that shape its structure and storytelling. Let's take a closer look at these foundational elements:

1. Plot

The plot is the sequence of events that makes up the story. It's essentially the novel's backbone, guiding the reader through various happenings, challenges, and resolutions. Some novels follow a linear plot, moving smoothly from one event to the next, while others might use flashbacks or even non-linear storytelling to keep things interesting.

For example, in *1984* by George Orwell, the plot follows Winston Smith, a man living in a dystopian society ruled by a totalitarian regime. As the plot progresses, we see his growing resistance to the oppressive system, leading to moments of tension and eventual heartbreak.

2. Characters

Characters are the individuals (sometimes animals or even inanimate objects) that populate the novel's world. These characters drive the story forward, and their choices and development are central to the novel's plot. There are main characters, like protagonists, antagonists, and supporting characters, who help enrich the narrative.

In Harper Lee's *To Kill a Mockingbird,* Scout Finch, a young girl growing up in the American South, narrates the story. Through her eyes, we meet her father, Atticus, her brother, Jem, and other characters who illuminate themes of racial injustice and moral integrity.

3. Setting

The setting includes the time and place where the novel's events occur. A well-crafted setting can transport readers to different worlds- an actual historical period or an entirely fictional universe. The setting is often more than just a backdrop—it can influence the mood, tone, and characters' behaviour.

In J.R.R. Tolkien's *The Lord of the Rings*, the setting of Middle-earth is richly detailed, from the peaceful Shire to the dark lands of Mordor. The world Tolkien created is so vivid that it becomes a character in itself, shaping the adventures of the heroes.

4. Theme

The theme of a novel is its underlying message or the big ideas it explores. A novel can have multiple themes, ranging from love, power, and justice to more abstract concepts like human nature or the clash between good and evil. Themes give the novel emotional and intellectual depth, inviting readers to think beyond the plot and characters.

In *Pride and Prejudice* by Jane Austen, the themes of social class, marriage, and personal growth are central to the story. Through Elizabeth Bennet's journey, the novel explores the tension between societal expectations and individual happiness.

5. Point of View

The point of view determines who is telling the story and how much they know. A novel can be written in the first person (from a character's perspective), third person limited (where the narrator knows the thoughts of one or a few characters), or third person omniscient (where the narrator knows everything about all the characters and events).

For example, J.D. Salinger's The Catcher in the Rye is told from Holden Caulfield's first-person perspective. His personal reflections and emotional state create an intimate reading experience.

6. Conflict

Conflict is the driving force behind a novel's plot. It can be internal (within a character's mind) or external (between characters or between a character and their environment). Without conflict, there is no story—it keeps readers engaged, wanting to know how things will be resolved.

In Herman Melville's *Moby-Dick*, the conflict is external (Captain Ahab's obsessive hunt for the white whale) and internal (Ahab's struggle with vengeance). This dual-layered conflict adds depth to the narrative.

7. Style and Language

Authors' styles are the ways they use language to tell their stories. Some writers prefer a straightforward style, while others employ more complex language, metaphors, and symbols. The style affects the tone and pace of the novel, shaping how readers engage with the story.

Gabriel García Márquez's *One Hundred Years of Solitude* is an excellent example of a unique style. Márquez uses magical realism, blending the fantastical with the real to create a dreamlike atmosphere that adds to the novel's thematic richness.

Types of Novel

The novel, as a form of literature, offers a wide array of possibilities for storytelling. Its versatility allows for exploring different plots, settings, characters, and themes, making the novel a rich and diverse genre. From romantic tales to dystopian futures, from epic adventures to intimate portrayals of human emotions, the novel can encompass the entire range of human experience. This essay will delve into the various types of novels, discussing their defining characteristics and providing examples from world literature.

1. Literary Novels

Literary novels emphasise depth in character development, sophisticated language, and a focus on themes and ideas rather than fast-paced plots. Often regarded as high art, these novels prioritise intellectual and emotional engagement over entertainment, encouraging readers to reflect on human nature, society, and philosophical concepts.

Characteristics:

- Complex characters with deep emotional and psychological development
- Themes often related to the human condition, existentialism, and moral dilemmas

- Emphasis on language, style, and structure
- Often explores social and cultural issues

The Great Gatsby by F. Scott Fitzgerald

This novel explores themes of the American Dream, wealth, and social class through the tragic story of Jay Gatsby, whose relentless pursuit of success and love leads to his downfall. The novel is known for its rich symbolism, poetic language, and deep character analysis.

Crime and Punishment by Fyodor Dostoevsky

Dostoevsky's novel delves into the moral and psychological turmoil of Raskolnikov, a man who murders a pawnbroker only to be consumed by guilt and paranoia. The story explores themes of redemption, suffering, and justice, making it a hallmark of literary fiction.

2. Historical Novels

Historical novels are set in a particular period and often blend factual historical events with fictional characters and narratives. They allow readers to explore past societies, cultures, and significant historical events through the lens of personal stories.

Characteristics:

- Set in a past period (often at least 50 years before the writing of the novel)
- Incorporates historical figures, events, or settings
- Blends fictional characters and plots with accurate historical details
- Provides insight into the social, political, and cultural context of the time

War and Peace by Leo Tolstoy

This epic novel takes place during the Napoleonic Wars and follows the lives of several aristocratic families in Russia. Tolstoy masterfully intertwines historical events with the personal dramas of his characters, providing readers with both an intimate and panoramic view of history.

The Book Thief by Markus Zusak

Set during World War II, this novel follows a young girl named Liesel, who finds solace in stealing books while her foster family hides a Jewish man in their basement. The novel blends the horrors of the Holocaust with a personal story of love, loss, and the power of words.

3. Science Fiction Novels

Science fiction (sci-fi) novels explore futuristic or alternative realities, often involving advanced technology, space exploration, time travel, or extraterrestrial life. These novels frequently raise questions about the impact of technology and scientific advancements on human society and the nature of existence.

Characteristics:

- Futuristic or speculative settings
- Incorporation of advanced technology, space exploration, or alternative realities
- Exploration of societal, ethical, and philosophical issues related to science and technology
- Often set in dystopian or utopian worlds

1984 by George Orwell

This classic dystopian novel envisions a future where a totalitarian regime led by Big Brother controls every aspect of life. Through the protagonist Winston Smith, Orwell explores themes of surveillance, government control, and the loss of individuality, making it a staple of sci-fi literature.

Dune by Frank Herbert

Dune is set in the distant future on the desert planet of Arrakis, where politics, religion, and ecology intertwine. The novel explores themes of power, environmentalism, and human survival and has had a lasting influence on science fiction and popular culture.

4. Fantasy Novels

Fantasy novels transport readers to magical worlds filled with mythical creatures, supernatural elements, and epic quests. These novels often occur in imaginary settings and involve protagonists who face challenges that require bravery, wit, and sometimes magical abilities to overcome.

Characteristics:

- Set in imaginary or magical worlds
- Inclusion of supernatural elements, mythical creatures, or magical powers
- Epic quests or battles between good and evil
- Themes of heroism, destiny, and adventure

The Lord of the Rings by J.R.R. Tolkien

This epic fantasy trilogy follows Frodo Baggins as he embarks on a dangerous journey to destroy the One Ring and defeat the dark lord Sauron. The novel is rich in world-building, featuring detailed histories, languages, and cultures, and it explores themes of friendship, power, and sacrifice.

Harry Potter series by J.K. Rowling

Set in a magical world hidden within our own, the *Harry Potter* series follows the journey of a young boy who discovers he is a wizard. The novels explore themes of love, friendship, and the battle between good and evil, making them beloved by readers of all ages.

5. Romantic Novels

Romantic novels focus on the complexities of love and relationships. While some may delve into the idealised aspects of romance, others explore the emotional challenges and conflicts between lovers. These novels often emphasise personal growth, the power of love, and emotional connections.

Characteristics:

- Focus on romantic relationships between characters.
- Exploration of emotional and psychological aspects of love
- Themes of passion, desire, and conflict
- Often (but not always) conclude with a resolution of the romantic tension

Pride and Prejudice by Jane Austen

One of the most beloved romantic novels in English literature, *Pride and Prejudice,* follows Elizabeth Bennet and Mr. Darcy as they navigate misunderstandings, societal expectations, and their growing affection for each other. The novel explores themes of class, pride, and the transformative power of love.

Wuthering Heights by Emily Brontë

This Gothic romance centres around the passionate and destructive love between Heathcliff and Catherine Earnshaw. Set on the wild Yorkshire moors, the novel delves into themes of obsession, revenge, and the darker aspects of love.

6. Mystery and Crime Novels

Mystery and crime novels revolve around solving a puzzle, often a crime, with the protagonist (usually a detective or investigator) working to uncover the truth. These novels are frequently filled with suspense, twists, and unexpected revelations, keeping readers engaged until the final resolution.

Characteristics:

- Central plot revolves around a mystery, often a crime
- The protagonist works to solve the mystery through investigation and deduction
- Suspenseful, with plot twists and red herrings
- Themes of justice, morality, and human behaviour

The Hound of the Baskervilles by Sir Arthur Conan Doyle

One of the most famous Sherlock Holmes novels, *The Hound of the Baskervilles*, follows the legendary detective as he investigates the mysterious death of Sir Charles Baskerville, believed to have been caused by a supernatural hound. The novel combines elements of mystery, horror, and Gothic fiction.

Gone Girl by Gillian Flynn

This modern psychological thriller revolves around Amy Dunne's disappearance and the suspicion that falls on her husband, Nick. The novel delves into themes of deception, manipulation, and the complexities of marriage, offering readers a gripping and darkly twisted mystery.

7. Adventure Novels

Adventure novels focus on action, excitement, and exploration. They often involve a hero embarking on a journey of danger and discovery. These novels transport readers to exotic locations and challenge the protagonists with physical and moral obstacles.

Characteristics:

- Central focus on action, exploration, and adventure
- The protagonist embarks on a journey or quest
- Themes of bravery, survival, and discovery
- Often set in exotic or unfamiliar locations

Treasure Island by Robert Louis Stevenson

This classic adventure novel follows young Jim Hawkins as he embarks on a treacherous journey to find buried treasure. The novel is filled with pirates, treasure maps, and thrilling battles, making it a quintessential example of the adventure genre.

The Call of the Wild by Jack London

Set in the Klondike Gold Rush, *The Call of the Wild* follows a domesticated dog named Buck as he is thrust into the harsh wilderness of the Yukon. The novel explores themes of survival, instinct, and the primal call of nature.

8. Coming-of-age novels

Coming-of-age novels, also known as bildungsroman, focus on the psychological and moral growth of the protagonist, typically from childhood to adulthood. These novels explore the challenges of growing up, personal identity, and self-discovery.

Characteristics:

- Central focus on the protagonist's emotional and psychological growth
- Often explores themes of identity, self-discovery, and maturity
- The protagonist faces challenges related to adolescence or young adulthood

- Themes of rebellion, conformity, and personal development

The Catcher in the Rye by J.D. Salinger

This iconic coming-of-age novel follows Holden Caulfield as he navigates the complexities of adolescence, rebellion, and alienation. Holden's internal struggles and search for meaning in a disconnected world resonate deeply with young adult readers.

To Kill a Mockingbird by Harper Lee

Set in the racially charged American South, *To Kill a Mockingbird* is a coming-of-age story that follows Scout Finch as she witnesses her father, Atticus, defend a black man accused of raping a white woman. Through Scout's perspective, the novel explores themes of racism, justice, and morality.

9. Dystopian Novels

Dystopian novels are set in an imagined future or alternate reality where society has degraded into oppression, extreme control, or chaos. These novels often serve as social critiques, exploring totalitarianism, freedom, and individual vs. collective good themes.

Characteristics:

- Set in a future or alternate reality where society is dysfunctional or oppressive
- Themes of government control, loss of individual freedoms, and societal collapse
- Protagonists often rebel against societal norms or authorities
- Social and political critique is a crucial element

Brave New World by Aldous Huxley

Set in a future where society is controlled through genetic engineering, consumerism, and a rigid caste system, *Brave New World* explores themes of conformity, freedom, and the cost of happiness—the novel critiques modern society's reliance on technology and the pursuit of pleasure.

The Hunger Games by Suzanne Collins

Set in a dystopian future where the government holds annual death matches to maintain control, *The Hunger Games* follows Katniss Everdeen as she becomes a symbol of resistance against the oppressive regime. The novel explores themes of power, survival, and rebellion.

10. Gothic Novels

Gothic novels combine elements of horror, romance, and mystery. They are often set in dark, foreboding locations like castles or haunted houses. These novels create an atmosphere of suspense and dread, with characters confronting supernatural forces or psychological terror.

Characteristics:

- Dark, mysterious settings (often castles, mansions, or remote landscapes)
- Themes of fear, madness, and the supernatural
- Blurring of the lines between reality and the paranormal
- Often includes a heroine who faces psychological or physical peril

Dracula by Bram Stoker

This classic Gothic novel tells the story of Count Dracula's attempt to move from Transylvania to England and his encounters with those who seek to stop him. The book blends horror, romance, and suspense elements and is an iconic example of Gothic literature.

Jane Eyre by Charlotte Brontë

While primarily a romance, *Jane Eyre* also incorporates Gothic elements, particularly in portraying the mysterious Thornfield Hall and its secrets. The novel explores identity, independence, and love themes in a dark, eerie atmosphere.

Novels come in various types, each offering unique ways to tell stories and explore themes. Whether it's the emotional depth of a literary novel, the excitement of an adventure, or the speculative intrigue of science fiction, novels can transport readers to different worlds and offer fresh perspectives on life. Understanding the various types of novels can enhance our appreciation of this versatile and captivating literary form.

CHAPTER I

From Oral Traditions to the Birth of the Novel

"The journey from oral traditions to the birth of the novel is a fascinating exploration of how stories have evolved. From ancient storytellers who relied solely on memory to the printed word that democratised literature, the transformation is marked by various cultural and technological shifts. Oral storytelling has always been a vital part of human civilisation, serving as more than just entertainment but a means to preserve history, teach moral lessons and reinforce social norms. The shared experience of listening to a storyteller created strong community bonds, making each tale an integral part of the collective memory."

This chapter will delve into the rich history of oral storytelling traditions from diverse cultures worldwide and examine how these oral narratives laid the groundwork for written stories. You'll explore the techniques employed by oral storytellers—like repetition and rhythm—and how these elements influenced early written works. We will also discuss the monumental shift brought about by the advent of written language, citing examples like Homer's epic poems, which transitioned from oral recitations to transcribed texts. By tracing these developmental stages, this chapter aims to illuminate the foundational influences that have shaped the modern novel as a literary form.

The Role of Oral Storytelling Traditions

Oral storytelling, with a history that dates back thousands of years, has been the foundation for many cultural traditions. These stories, far from being mere entertainment, have preserved history, moral lessons, and shared experiences within a community. In various cultures worldwide, oral traditions have acted as communal glue, reinforcing social norms and values and creating a sense of unity among listeners. They have been instrumental in preserving each community's unique identity and continuity over time.

For instance, the griots of West Africa, who have been the keepers of oral tradition for centuries, recited epic narratives, genealogies, and historical accounts. They effectively functioned as living repositories of their culture's collective memory. Similarly, Native American tribes used oral storytelling to pass down creation myths, legends, and spiritual teachings from one generation to the next. These stories shared within the community, reinforced social norms and values and created a sense of unity among listeners.

The techniques employed in oral storytelling also played a crucial role in shaping narrative forms seen in modern novels. One such technique is repetition, which helps storytellers remember lengthy tales and emphasise essential points for the audience. Characters' actions, events, or phrases might be repeated to reinforce their significance within the story. Repetition can also be found in modern literature, where authors use it to highlight key themes or motifs.

Another technique frequently employed in oral narration is rhythm. By incorporating a rhythmic structure into their stories, storytellers made their narratives more engaging and accessible. This rhythm-influenced prose style leads to a more fluid and dynamic form of storytelling, which can still be observed in contemporary novels. For instance, the lyrical quality of Toni Morrison's prose demonstrates how rhythm elevates a narrative's emotional depth and resonance.

As societies transitioned from oral to written cultures, how stories were recorded and disseminated changed dramatically. The advent of written language allowed for the documentation of previously oral narratives, ensuring their preservation for future generations. This shift was monumental, enabling stories to transcend the limitations of memory and geography.

In ancient Greece, the works of Homer, such as "The Iliad" and "The Odyssey," are prime examples of how oral tradition influenced written literature. These epics were initially passed down through generations by word of mouth before being transcribed into written form. The transition allowed these timeless tales to reach a wider audience and laid the groundwork for the Western literary canon.

The influence of oral traditions on written narratives did not stop there. Many structural elements in modern novels echo the roots of oral storytelling. For instance, the episodic nature of oral tales—where stories are told in segments or episodes—can be seen in the serialised storytelling of Charles Dickens's novels. Dickens often published his works in instalments, keeping readers eagerly anticipating the next chapter, much like audiences awaited the continuation of an oral tale.

Moreover, using archetypal characters and universal themes in oral traditions has left a lasting legacy on novelistic structures. Archetypes such as the hero, the mentor, and the trickster appear across various cultures' oral stories and continue to populate the pages of contemporary fiction. Joseph Campbell's concept of the "hero's journey," which outlines a typical narrative arc shared by many myths and stories, illustrates this enduring influence. Modern novels like J.K. Rowling's "Harry Potter" series utilise similar character archetypes and thematic structures, demonstrating the ongoing relevance of oral storytelling conventions.

The dialogic nature of oral traditions, where interaction between the storyteller and the audience is integral, is also reflected in the style of certain modern novels. Writers like James Joyce and Virginia Woolf employ stream-of-consciousness techniques that mimic oral narratives' fluid, conversational style. This approach invites readers to actively engage with the text, similar to how audiences participated in oral storytelling sessions.

Additionally, the social functions of oral storytelling have parallels in how contemporary novels address cultural and societal issues. Just as oral narratives convey moral lessons and social values, novels often serve as a medium for exploring and critiquing social norms and injustices. For instance, Harper Lee's "To Kill a Mockingbird" addresses themes of racial inequality and moral integrity, mirroring the way oral stories imparted ethical guidance.

Impact of Classical Epics and Myths

The influence of classical literature on the development of the novel is profound and multifaceted. Classical epics provided a treasure trove of universal themes and archetypal characters that continue to resonate in modern novels. These narratives often revolved around fundamental human experiences, such as love and conflict, heroism and betrayal, which are still central themes in contemporary storytelling.

Take Homer's "The Iliad" and "The Odyssey," for example. These epic poems are rich with timeless themes like the struggle between good and evil, the complexities of fate, and the pursuit of glory. The characters in these stories are archetypes we encounter repeatedly: the noble hero, the cunning trickster, the wise mentor, and others. These archetypes form the backbone of countless modern stories, providing a familiar framework for authors to build their tales. Such universal themes and characters help readers connect with the story on a deeper emotional level, making the narrative more engaging and relatable.

Furthermore, the narrative structure of classical literature offered early blueprints for constructing compelling plots. Epics often feature complex, multi-layered storylines with various subplots and character arcs that converge into a cohesive whole. This structuring method is evident in works like Virgil's "Aeneid," which follows its protagonist through numerous trials and tribulations, weaving together personal struggles with larger-than-life adventures. Such sophisticated plotting techniques have influenced many modern novels, where multiple storylines and perspectives are artistically interwoven to create rich, intricate narratives.

Classical literature also serves as a reflection of the cultural beliefs, societal norms, and historical contexts of its time. Myths and epics encapsulate the values and traditions of ancient societies, offering insights into how people lived, what they believed, and how they understood the world around them. For instance, the Greek myths reveal much about ancient Greek society, including their views on gods, fate, and human nature. The cultural reflection in these works helps readers understand the historical context that shaped the narratives, adding depth and nuance to the stories. This cultural layer enriches the reading experience, allowing modern readers to explore the plot and the philosophical and societal fabric of the past.

Additionally, many novels, especially fantasy ones, draw direct inspiration from classical myths. J.R.R. Tolkien's "The Lord of the Rings" is heavily influenced by Norse and Germanic mythology, while Rick Riordan's "Percy Jackson" series brings Greek mythology to life in a contemporary setting. By reimagining these ancient stories, authors can create fresh, exciting narratives that still carry the weight and significance of their mythological origins. These adaptations often fascinate readers because they offer a blend of familiarity and novelty—new stories built on the enduring foundation of classic myths.

Medieval Romance and Allegory

Medieval literature played a significant role in shaping modern novels' narrative forms and themes. This influence can be traced through various elements widely prevalent during medieval times, each contributing uniquely to the evolution of literary storytelling.

One of the most prominent contributions of medieval literature to modern narrative forms is the introduction of chivalric themes. Medieval romances often revolved around noble ideals, love, and adventures undertaken by knights and heroes. These stories highlighted virtues such as honour, bravery, and loyalty, presenting protagonists who embodied these ideals. The Arthurian legends, for example, feature characters like King Arthur and Sir Lancelot, whose quests and moral dilemmas laid the groundwork for character-driven narratives in later novels. This emphasis on personal honour and romantic love has persisted into contemporary literature, where complex characters driven by their ideals and emotions continue to captivate readers.

The use of allegory is another significant contribution from medieval literature that has influenced novelistic themes and narrative techniques. Allegorical narratives allowed medieval writers to convey moral and spiritual lessons through symbolic storytelling. One of the most famous examples is "The Divine Comedy" by Dante Alighieri, which uses the journey through Hell, Purgatory, and Heaven as an allegory for the soul's path towards God. Another notable work is "Piers Plowman" by William Langland, which delves into righteousness and social justice themes. These allegories provided a framework for exploring more profound human experiences and abstract concepts, a practice that continues in modern fiction. Even today, many novels embed allegorical layers within their plots to offer insight into broader societal and ethical concerns.

The concept of courtly love introduced intricate emotional dynamics between characters, influencing how relationships are portrayed in novels. Courtly love, as depicted in the works of troubadours and poets like Chrétien de Troyes, described an idealised and often unattainable form of love that emphasised chivalry, secrecy, and the ennobling effects of loving someone from afar. These stories featured elaborate love triangles, unrequited passions, and the tension between duty and desire. Such narrative elements have become staples in romantic fiction and drama, adding depth to character interactions and driving plot development. The exploration of complex emotional states and the nuanced portrayal of relationships in medieval literature laid the foundation for the rich psychological landscapes found in contemporary novels.

Persistence of form is yet another way medieval literature has influenced modern storytelling. Elements of medieval narrative structures, such as episodic adventures and quests, have made their way into later prose forms. Medieval epics like "Beowulf" and "The Song of Roland" are interconnected tales and present a model for structuring long-form narratives. This episodic format allows for the development of multi-faceted characters and expansive worlds, a technique evident in modern serialised novels and series. With its clear objectives and transformative journeys, the quest motif has remained a popular plot device, underpinning genres ranging from fantasy to science fiction. Stories like J.R.R. Tolkien's "The Lord of the Rings" and George R.R. Martin's "A Game of Thrones" echo the structure and themes of medieval quests, illustrating the lasting impact of these early narrative forms.

The Rise of the Chivalric Novel

The emergence of the chivalric novel marked a significant point in the development of literary forms and storytelling. Rooted deeply in the cultural context of chivalry, these novels reflected the society in which they were born. During the Middle Ages, chivalry was a social code and a way of life that elevated ideals such as bravery, honour, and gallantry. Knights, with their shining armour and noble quests, became symbols of these virtues. This valorisation of chivalric ideals coincided with a burgeoning interest in heroic narratives, setting a fertile ground for the birth of the chivalric novel.

The cultural context of chivalry provided a rich tapestry of themes and values ripe for literature exploration. As society glorified the traits associated with knights, there was a growing appetite for stories celebrating these qualities. The chivalric novel responded to this demand by weaving tales of adventure, love, and heroism that captured readers' imaginations. These stories often featured protagonists who embodied the highest ideals of chivalry, embarking on quests to prove their worth and uphold justice. In many ways, the chivalric novel served as both an escapist fantasy and a moral compass, offering readers a vision of a world where virtues triumphed over vices.

One of the most striking contributions of the chivalric novel to literary forms is its approach to character development. Unlike earlier literature, where characters were often one-dimensional and driven by external factors, the chivalric novel introduced nuanced character arcs. Protagonists in these stories were deeply influenced by their virtues and vices, making them more relatable and complex. For example, Sir Lancelot, one of the most famous knights of Arthurian legend, is portrayed not only as a paragon of bravery and skill but also as a flawed human being struggling with his love for Queen Guinevere. This duality made characters in chivalric novels more compelling and provided a template for future authors to create multifaceted heroes and heroines.

In addition to character development, chivalric novels profoundly influenced plot structures in literature. These stories frequently employed quests and adventures as central plot devices, establishing patterns still utilised in modern novels. A classic example is "Le Morte d'Arthur" by Sir Thomas Malory, which recounts the various quests undertaken by the Knights of the Round Table. Each quest serves as a narrative vehicle through which characters confront challenges, grow, and ultimately achieve or fail in their endeavours. This episodic structure allowed multiple storylines to be woven, creating a rich and expansive narrative tapestry. Such techniques have been adapted and refined over centuries, forming the backbone of countless literary works across genres.

Moreover, the legacy of the chivalric novel extends far beyond its medieval origins. While some critics may view these novels as relics of a bygone era, their themes resonate in contemporary literature, particularly fantasy and romance. The trope of the knight-errant embarking on a perilous journey remains a staple in modern storytelling. From J.R.R. Tolkien's "The Lord of the Rings" to George R.R. Martin's "A Song of Ice and Fire," the influence of chivalric ideals and narrative structures is evident. Even in romance novels, the emphasis on noble love and the obstacles that lovers must overcome harken back to the courtly love traditions celebrated in chivalric literature.

Furthermore, the thematic richness of chivalric novels has left an indelible mark on literary and popular culture. The ideals of honour, bravery, and self-sacrifice that underpin these stories continue to inspire new generations of writers and readers. Characters like King Arthur and his knights have become archetypes, their tales retold and reimagined in various forms of media, from books and films to television shows and video games. The enduring appeal of these stories lies in their ability to speak to universal human experiences and aspirations, providing timeless lessons about courage, loyalty, and the pursuit of a higher purpose.

Even though the world has changed dramatically since the age of chivalry, the core values espoused by chivalric novels remain relevant. In a time when cynicism and disillusionment can easily take hold, these stories offer a beacon of hope and a reminder of the potential for goodness within us all. They encourage us to strive for excellence, to face our inner demons, and to act with integrity and compassion. In this sense, the chivalric novel is not merely a historical artefact but a living tradition that continues to shape our understanding of what it means to be truly noble.

Transition from Manuscript to Print Culture

One of the most pivotal moments in the evolution of the novel was the transition from manuscript culture to print. Johannes Gutenberg's invention of the printing press in the mid-15th century marked the dawn of a new era in literature. This technological advancement revolutionised how stories were disseminated, making literature accessible to a broader audience than ever before.

Before the printing press, manuscripts were laboriously hand-copied by scribes. This painstaking process meant that books were rare and expensive, accessible only to the elite and those within religious or academic institutions. As a result, the spread of ideas and stories was slow and limited. The invention of the printing press changed all that. Suddenly, it was possible to produce multiple copies of a text quickly and efficiently, drastically reducing costs and increasing availability. Literature began to reach a much wider audience, breaking down barriers between different social classes.

This newfound accessibility had a profound impact on literary forms. With more people able to read, there was a growing demand for diverse types of literature. Writers began experimenting with new styles and genres, creating a richer and more varied literary landscape. Poetry, which had dominated manuscript culture, started to share the stage with prose fiction. Early novels, such as Thomas More's "Utopia" and Miguel de Cervantes' "Don Quixote," emerged during this period, reflecting readers' changing tastes and interests.

In addition, the spread of printed works facilitated cultural and intellectual exchange on an unprecedented scale. Ideas could now travel across countries and continents, influencing and enriching local cultures. The Renaissance, characterised by a renewed interest in classical learning and humanism, was partly fueled by the proliferation of printed texts. Scholars could engage more easily with each other's work, fostering a vibrant intellectual community. Literary movements and philosophies spread rapidly, shaping narratives and storytelling techniques.

As printed works became more common, there was also a significant shift in the concept of authorship. Many works were anonymous or attributed to patrons rather than writers in the manuscript era. With the advent of print, authors started to gain recognition and establish their identities and reputations as storytellers. This emergence of authorial identity allowed writers to carve out distinct voices and styles, contributing to developing individualistic and personal narratives characteristic of novels.

This period also saw the rise of the professional writer. The possibility of reaching a large readership created new economic opportunities for authors. Writers like Daniel Defoe and Samuel Richardson could make a living from their craft, furthering the establishment of the novel as a legitimate and respected literary form. The publication of serialised novels in newspapers and magazines became a popular way for authors to build their reputations and connect with readers, creating a sense of anticipation and engagement that is still seen today in modern publishing.

Moreover, the standardisation brought about by print technology helped to preserve texts accurately. Manuscript culture was prone to errors and variations, as each copy was unique. Print technology ensured that every printed book copy was identical, maintaining the integrity of the author's original work. This consistency helped establish a stable canon of literature that generations of readers could study, critique, and enjoy.

The shift from manuscript to print impacted written texts and the act of reading itself. As printed books became more affordable, private reading became increasingly popular. In contrast to the communal and oral nature of medieval manuscript readings, individuals could now enjoy literature in solitude, allowing for a more reflective and personal engagement with the text. This change in reading habits influenced the narrative techniques employed by writers, who began to delve deeper into character psychology and complex plot structures, knowing that their readers could take the time to savour and contemplate their works.

While the printing press democratised access to literature, it also led to the creation of literary markets and the phenomenon of bestsellers. With more books available, competition among titles grew fierce. Publishers and booksellers played crucial roles in promoting works and shaping literary tastes. Popular novels often reflected societal trends and issues, providing insight into the lives and concerns of ordinary people. This commercial aspect of printing further pushed authors to innovate and cater to the evolving preferences of their audience.

What We Learnt

Exploring the origins and early influences of the novel takes us on a journey through the rich tapestry of oral storytelling traditions, classical epics, and medieval literature. Throughout the chapter, we have seen how ancient storytellers used techniques like repetition and rhythm to captivate their audiences and preserve cultural narratives. These methods kept stories alive and shaped how modern novels are structured and told. From the epic tales of Homer to the episodic adventures in Dickens' serialised works, the legacy of these early forms continues to resonate in contemporary storytelling.

The transition from oral to written culture marked a significant turning point, allowing stories to be recorded and shared beyond their original communities. Classical literature provided timeless themes and archetypal characters that have become central to modern narratives. Meanwhile, the ideals of chivalry in medieval romances introduced complex character development and influential plot structures today. Finally, the shift from manuscript to print culture democratised access to literature, transforming how stories were consumed and paving the way for the novel to flourish. Understanding these early influences helps us appreciate the depth and diversity of the novel as a literary form and its ability to connect us across time and cultures.

CHAPTER II

The Evolution of the Novel

"The novel as a literary form has undergone remarkable transformations from the Renaissance to the Enlightenment period. Humanism and individualism began to shape literature during the Renaissance, encouraging writers to delve deeper into human experiences and emotions. Novels started to feature characters with complex personalities and internal conflicts, moving away from the formulaic storytelling of the medieval period. This shift allowed for a richer exploration of themes like personal growth, moral dilemmas, and self-discovery, which resonated deeply with readers."

In this chapter, we will journey through the evolution of the novel during these transformative periods. We will trace how humanist principles influenced character development and narrative styles, making stories more engaging and intellectually stimulating. Additionally, we'll explore the impact of individualism on narrative techniques, such as the emergence of stream-of-consciousness writing. The chapter then transitions to the Enlightenment period, highlighting how authors built on Renaissance foundations to address themes of reason, personal freedom, and social justice. We will understand how novels evolved to reflect and influence their times' cultural and intellectual currents by examining critical literary works and their socio-political contexts.

Humanism and Individualism in Literature

Humanism and individualism played critical roles in transforming literary works during the Renaissance. These intellectual movements emphasised the value of human beings and individual agency, profoundly influencing the portrayal of characters and themes in novels. The Humanist Movement, which emerged in the 14th century, firmly focused on personal experience and moral philosophy. Figures such as Erasmus were central to this movement, advocating for an education system grounded in classical literature and ethical reasoning. Erasmus's emphasis on personal experience and the inner life of individuals encouraged writers to delve deeper into the complexities of human nature.

The shift towards individualism allowed authors to explore more personal and subjective narrative styles. This was a departure from the often rigid and formulaic storytelling of the medieval period. Novels began to feature complex human emotions and psychological depth, presenting characters with distinct personalities and internal conflicts. For instance, individualism opened the way for diverse perspectives and voices, enriching the narrative tapestry. Writers were no longer confined to universal archetypes; instead, they could create multifaceted characters that resonated with readers' experiences.

The influence of humanism extended beyond character development to encompass plot structure and thematic exploration. Humanist ideas often led to stories centred around personal growth, moral dilemmas, and self-discovery. Characters embarked on journeys that mirrored their internal transformations, grappling with ethical questions and seeking personal fulfilment. This introspective approach resulted in narratives that were not only entertaining but also intellectually stimulating. Readers could engage with the text more profoundly, contemplating their values and beliefs through the characters' experiences.

One notable example of humanism's impact on literature is in Giovanni Boccaccio's works. His "Decameron," a collection of novellas written in the 14th century, exemplifies how humanist principles influenced storytelling. The "Decameron" features diverse characters with unique traits and motivations. The stories explore themes of love, virtue, and fortune, reflecting the complexity of human existence. Boccaccio's emphasis on individual experience and moral ambiguity set a precedent for future novelists, paving the way for more nuanced portrayals of human nature.

Individualism also contributed to developing narrative techniques highlighting human experience's subjectivity. Stream-of-consciousness writing, which emerged much later but has roots in Renaissance individualism, allows readers to immerse themselves in a character's thoughts and emotions. This technique creates an intimate connection between the reader and the character, facilitating a deeper understanding of the character's psyche. By presenting fragmented and nonlinear narratives, authors can capture the fluidity and unpredictability of human thought.

Renaissance humanism laid the groundwork for later literary movements, ensuring the enduring relevance of individual agency in literature. The focus on personal experience and moral philosophy resonated with writers and readers alike. During the Enlightenment, for instance, the emphasis on reason and individual rights built upon humanist foundations. Authors like Daniel Defoe and Samuel Richardson explored personal freedom and social justice themes, furthering the humanist tradition.

Moreover, the legacy of Renaissance humanism is evident in contemporary novels. Modern authors often grapple with questions of identity, morality, and self-discovery, echoing the concerns of their Renaissance predecessors. The rise of the psychological novel in the 19th and 20th centuries, with writers like Fyodor Dostoevsky and Virginia Woolf, demonstrates the lasting impact of humanist ideals. These authors delved into the intricacies of the human mind, exploring the complexities of consciousness and the challenges of self-understanding.

The Humanist Movement's emphasis on the individual's worth and potential sparked a significant evolution in literary themes. Writers began to focus on the human condition, exploring aspects such as ambition, passion, and ethical choices. This introspective turn made literature a mirror reflecting societal changes and philosophical inquiries of the time. With a newfound interest in personal narratives, novels depicted characters in a more realistic and relatable manner.

Individualism facilitated the creation of protagonists who embodied personal struggles and triumphs. These characters became vehicles for expressing broader human truths, making literature a medium for readers to examine their lives. The subjective nature of these narratives allowed for an exploration of inner conflicts and aspirations, mirroring the complexities of real-life experiences. This shift made stories more prosperous and engaging, providing readers with protagonists they could relate to and learn from.

Furthermore, Renaissance humanism's impact on literature was not limited to thematic content; it also revolutionised the structure of stories. The traditional linear plot gave way to more dynamic forms of storytelling. Plots became multi-layered, weaving together various subplots that reflected the interconnectedness of individual experiences. This complexity added depth to the narrative, encouraging readers to consider multiple perspectives and interpretations.

A clear example of this influence is evident in William Shakespeare's works. Although primarily known for his plays, Shakespeare's contributions to narrative structure and literary character development are immeasurable. His ability to integrate humanist principles into his works allowed him to create timeless characters that continue to resonate with readers. Characters like Hamlet and Macbeth embody the Renaissance fascination with personal agency and the consequences of moral choices, making them enduring subjects of study.

The Influence of the Printing Press

The advent of the printing press marked a pivotal moment in the evolution of literature and society. Introduced by Johannes Gutenberg in the mid-15th century, the printing press revolutionised the production and consumption of novels during the Renaissance and Enlightenment periods. This revolutionary technology transformed how books were made and profoundly affected societal structures and cultural landscapes.

Before the printing press, books were laboriously hand-copied by scribes, which made them rare and expensive commodities accessible only to the affluent. The introduction of the printing press drastically reduced the cost of book production, leading to a wider dissemination of literature. For the first time, books became accessible to a broader audience, including the emerging middle class. As a result, more people could afford books, increasing literacy rates. This democratisation of knowledge fostered an intellectually curious and literate society that valued education and self-improvement.

Authors experienced a significant transformation in their roles as well. Before the printing press, authors often remained anonymous or received little recognition for their work. The repeatability and distribution capabilities of the printing press allowed writers to reach larger audiences, gaining widespread recognition and celebrated status. This newfound fame empowered authors as public figures, enabling them to influence social and political thought. Consequently, diverse voices and narratives emerged, reflecting various experiences and perspectives. Authors from different backgrounds started addressing themes pertinent to their lives and times, enriching the literary landscape with new ideas and storytelling techniques.

The standardisation of texts was another critical impact of the printing press. Before its advent, variations in hand-copied manuscripts led to inconsistencies and errors. The printing process brought uniformity and consistency to published works, ensuring that readers received the same content regardless of where they bought the book. This standardisation influenced readers' expectations of quality and style, establishing benchmarks for literary excellence. Over time, it preserved literary forms and genres, contributing to developing a shared cultural heritage. Readers began to expect specific structural and linguistic standards, which helped shape the evolution of the novel as a distinct literary form.

Furthermore, the printing press acted as a catalyst for literary movements. Once confined to the elite, literature reflected the evolving social and cultural landscapes. The increased availability of books meant that ideas could be disseminated quickly and widely. This facilitated the spread of Renaissance humanism, emphasising individual potential and experience. Writers like Erasmus and Thomas More utilised print to advocate for educational reform and moral philosophy, impacting the intellectual elite and the broader populace. Similarly, the Enlightenment's focus on reason, scientific inquiry, and human rights found fertile ground in the printed word. Novels of this period began to incorporate these themes, exploring new narrative styles and philosophical ideas.

In turn, these literary movements influenced social norms and cultural practices. For instance, the rise of the novel as a popular literary form during the 17th and 18th centuries can be attributed to the interplay between the printing press and emerging social values. Novels provide a platform for exploring complex human emotions and social dynamics, resonating with readers' experiences. Characters were portrayed with psychological depth, and plots often revolved around personal growth, moral dilemmas, and societal critique. These innovative narrative styles entertained and prompted readers to reflect on their lives and world.

As the printing press made literature more accessible, it spurred debates about censorship and intellectual freedom. Authorities recognised the power of printed works to shape public opinion and control information. Various forms of censorship were implemented to restrict the dissemination of specific ideas. However, the very nature of print enabled resistance against such restrictions. Underground publications and clandestine printing presses emerged, allowing dissenting voices to be heard. This dynamic tension between control and freedom underscored the transformative potential of the printing press in shaping societal discourse.

The impact of the printing press extended beyond literature to other forms of media and communication. Newspapers, pamphlets, and periodicals flourished, providing timely information and facilitating public debate. The spread of printed materials contributed to exchanging ideas across geographic and cultural boundaries, fostering a sense of interconnectedness among societies. Intellectuals and scholars could engage in dialogues transcending physical distances, advancing knowledge and innovation.

Despite the initial focus on religious and scholarly texts, the printing press eventually embraced various genres and subjects, further broadening its reach. Popular fiction, travelogues, scientific treatises, and philosophical essays all found their way into print. This diversity of content catered to varied interests and tastes, enriching the reading experience for individuals from different walks of life. The proliferation of printed works also encouraged the establishment of libraries and reading societies, creating communal spaces for intellectual engagement and social interaction.

Pioneering Authors and Their Works

When examining the evolution of the novel from the Renaissance to the Enlightenment, it is essential to recognise the contributions of Miguel de Cervantes, Daniel Defoe, Samuel Richardson, and Henry Fielding. These authors crafted compelling narratives and pioneered techniques and themes that shaped literature's trajectory.

Miguel de Cervantes' "Don Quixote," published in two parts (1605 and 1615), is widely regarded as one of the first modern novels. Cervantes masterfully merged realism with fantasy, creating a world where the protagonist's delusions blend seamlessly with the mundane reality around him. Don Quixote's adventures reflect critique and celebration of chivalric traditions, thus setting a precedent for exploring complex narrative techniques. The novel's structure, which interweaves multiple perspectives and stories within stories, challenges readers to consider the fluid boundaries between reality and illusion. Cervantes employed satire to comment on social norms, poking fun at the rigid societal structures of his time. By doing so, he established a framework for future novelists to explore identity, perception, and morality themes.

Following Cervantes, Daniel Defoe made a significant impact with "Robinson Crusoe" (1719). This novel encapsulates the values of the Enlightenment, emphasising individualism, perseverance, and economic activity. Crusoe's tale of survival on a deserted island highlights human ingenuity and the triumph of reason over adversity. Defoe brought a sense of realism to his narrative through meticulous detail, making readers feel they were experiencing Crusoe's struggles firsthand. "Robinson Crusoe" illustrates Enlightenment ideals by portraying a protagonist who embodies self-reliance and personal responsibility. Defoe's focus on practical knowledge and resourcefulness reflects the period's shifting attitudes toward human potential and progress. Moreover, the novel explores themes of colonialism and cultural encounters, providing a nuanced commentary on the expanding European influence during the era.

Samuel Richardson introduced a new narrative form with his epistolary novel, "Pamela, or Virtue Rewarded" (1740). By presenting the story through a series of letters the protagonist wrote, Richardson offered an intimate look into Pamela's thoughts and emotions. This format allowed for deep character exploration, particularly of female consciousness and virtue. Richardson's epistolary style added emotional depth and psychological complexity to the narrative, engaging readers in Pamela's plight and moral dilemmas. The novel's emphasis on marriage, social class, and virtue sparked widespread debate, prompting discussions about gender roles and societal expectations. "Pamela" influenced subsequent writers and resonated with readers across different social strata, highlighting the evolving public interest in personal and domestic issues.

Henry Fielding's "Tom Jones" (1749) stands as another monumental work in the development of the novel. Fielding utilised satire to examine social issues and moral ambiguity, offering a broad critique of eighteenth-century British society. The novel's sprawling narrative follows the life and adventures of Tom Jones, an illegitimate child, as he navigates various trials and tribulations. Through a diverse array of characters—ranging from the virtuous to the evil—Fielding illustrated the complexities of human behaviour and societal interactions. His humorous and often irreverent tone invited readers to question established norms and consider alternative viewpoints. Fielding's innovative narrative structure, with its omniscient narrator and direct addresses to the audience, broke new ground in storytelling, influencing the novel's evolution as a literary form.

Each of these authors made distinct contributions to the development of the novel, reflecting and shaping the cultural and intellectual currents of their respective periods. Cervantes' blending of realism and fantasy set the stage for narrative experimentation, while Defoe's emphasis on individualism and realism aligned with Enlightenment values. Richardson's introspective epistolary format provided a new means of character exploration, and Fielding's satirical approach expanded the novel's capacity for social critique.

Through their works, Cervantes, Defoe, Richardson, and Fielding demonstrated the novel's potential as a vehicle for exploring human experiences, societal norms, and philosophical ideas. Their innovations in narrative technique, characterisation, and thematic exploration paved the way for future generations of novelists. Understanding these contributions allows us to appreciate the novel's dynamic evolution and enduring impact on literature and culture.

Socio-Political Context of the Enlightenment

The Enlightenment, a period spanning the late 17th to 18th centuries, was marked by significant intellectual and socio-political transformations. These changes profoundly influenced novel writing. Central to this era was rationalism, which emphasised reason and scientific inquiry to understand and improve the world. Enlightenment thinkers believed that reason could combat ignorance, superstition, and tyranny, and these beliefs were vividly reflected in literature.

Authors began embedding characters with rational decision-making abilities. These characters often faced moral questions or social injustices, using logic and ethical reasoning to navigate their circumstances. Novels started addressing societal issues such as inequality, corruption, and human rights, framing these narratives within a context of rational thought. The protagonists' journeys required intellectual engagement from them and readers, who were encouraged to think critically about the plots and themes.

Political revolutions, most notably the American and French revolutions, profoundly impacted literary themes. These revolutions brought forth ideas of liberty, equality, and fraternity. Literature began exploring concepts of freedom and identity, often illustrating the struggle for independence and the quest for personal and collective rights. Characters in novels were depicted as revolutionaries or ordinary people caught in tumultuous times, grappling with questions of justice and autonomy. These narratives mirrored the more significant societal shifts towards democratic ideals and individual freedoms.

The works of philosophers like Jean-Jacques Rousseau and Voltaire also had a considerable influence on novelists. Rousseau's advocacy for natural human goodness and his criticism of societal constraints shaped literary discussions around human nature and societal reform. His belief in the fundamental right to freedom and autonomy inspired characters who broke away from traditional roles and sought self-fulfilment. Voltaire's sharp critiques of established institutions and his satirical style encouraged writers to explore and challenge power structures through their narratives. These philosophical influences led to complex character motivations and storylines questioning prevailing ideologies and norms.

Cultural transformations during the Enlightenment contributed significantly to literature alongside political and philosophical shifts. The rise of the middle class brought about new audiences who demanded stories reflecting their experiences and aspirations. This period saw increased literacy rates and book access, leading to a more diverse readership. Novelists began exploring themes relevant to the middle class, such as economic survival, social mobility, and family dynamics. Scientific advances during this era introduced new ways of understanding the human condition, influencing novelists to incorporate realism and emotional complexity elements into their works.

The changing cultural landscape allowed for more intricate and emotionally driven narratives. Authors experimented with different forms and styles, creating multi-layered characters who experienced various emotions and conflicts. These stories reflected the evolving social fabric, portraying the struggles and triumphs of individuals navigating a rapidly changing world. The inclusion of scientific perspectives brought a sense of realism to the novels, grounding fantastical elements in believable contexts.

What We Learnt

The journey through the development of novels from the Renaissance to the Enlightenment has shown how humanism and individualism reshaped literature. By emphasising personal experience and moral philosophy, humanist ideas allowed writers to explore more profound aspects of human nature, crafting characters with rich psychological depth. This shift gave rise to more personal and subjective narrative styles, moving away from the rigid storytelling of the medieval period. The Renaissance opened doors to complex emotional portrayals and diverse perspectives, leading readers into a world filled with unique characters and thought-provoking themes.

Entering the Enlightenment, the printing press played a crucial role in making literature accessible to wider audiences, democratising knowledge and reflecting societal changes. Key authors like Cervantes, Defoe, Richardson, and Fielding contributed significantly to the evolution of the novel, introducing new techniques and themes that addressed contemporary socio-political contexts. Rationalism, reason, and scientific inquiry became central to storytelling, embedding characters with logical decision-making skills and tackling issues of freedom and justice. These innovations laid the groundwork for modern narratives, underlining the profound impact of humanist and Enlightenment values on literature.

CHAPTER III

19th Century Novels

"Exploring 19th-century novels reveals a fascinating dichotomy between Realism and Romanticism, two significant literary movements that shaped the period's literature. Romantic novels, with their emotionally charged narratives, drew readers into the depths of human emotions through intense stories and vivid descriptions of nature. This movement emphasised individualism and heroism and often incorporated fantastical elements to explore deeper truths about existence and human experience. In contrast, Realism emerged as a response to these grandiose tales, focusing on the ordinary lives of everyday people with meticulous attention to detail and a critical eye towards societal norms."

This chapter delves into how Romantic and Realist authors portrayed life through their unique perspectives and techniques. It examines Romantic literature's emotionally rich and passionate themes, showcasing how authors like Mary Shelley and Emily Brontë used nature and supernatural elements to reflect their characters' inner lives. On the other hand, it also highlights the rise of Realism, emphasising how writers like Charles Dickens and Gustave Flaubert turned their pens towards social commentary, detailed settings, and complex, relatable characters. By understanding these contrasting approaches, readers can gain insight into the diverse ways 19th-century novelists captured the essence of their time.

Characteristics of Romantic Novels

In the 19th century, Romantic novels brought a fresh perspective to literature, characterised by their emotionally charged narratives. Authors like Mary Shelley and Emily Brontë created stories that immersed readers deeply in the character's emotional lives. These narratives often caused readers to reflect on their experiences and emotions, fostering a personal connection with the text. By emphasising intense feelings and passions, Romantic novels provided a sharp contrast to the more restrained storytelling styles that had preceded them.

The depiction of nature in Romantic literature played a significant role in symbolising freedom and idealism. Nature was not just a backdrop but an active participant in the storyline, reflecting the characters' inner lives and setting the stage for their struggles and triumphs. For instance, in "Wuthering Heights," Emily Brontë uses the wild, untamed moors to mirror the tumultuous relationship between Heathcliff and Catherine. This connection between humans and nature allowed readers to experience the story on multiple levels and understand the characters' struggles more profoundly.

Individualism and heroism were central themes in Romantic novels, focusing on protagonists who challenged societal norms and inspired readers to value personal freedom. Characters such as Victor Frankenstein in Mary Shelley's "Frankenstein" or Jane Eyre in Charlotte Brontë's eponymous novel embody this spirit of individualism. They defy societal expectations and pursue their paths regardless of the consequences. These characters' journeys highlight the importance of personal liberty and the courage required to uphold one's beliefs, encouraging readers to question societal constraints and appreciate the power of self-determination.

Moreover, the incorporation of fantasy and supernatural elements in Romantic novels broadened the scope of storytelling, inviting readers to explore metaphorical meanings and more profound truths. Works like "Frankenstein" and "Gothic tales" often included supernatural elements like monsters, ghosts, and otherworldly occurrences. These fantastical components allowed authors to delve into complex themes such as the limits of human knowledge, the consequences of ambition, and the nature of existence. By using the supernatural, Romantic writers could address these topics creatively and engagingly, capturing readers' imaginations and encouraging them to think beyond the ordinary.

Realist Depiction of Everyday Life

The 19th century was a transformative period for literature, with Realism emerging as a significant movement that dramatically altered the landscape of novels. Realism aimed to portray life accurately without embellishment, providing readers insights into everyday experiences and social conditions. This shift in focus brought about several notable changes in how stories were told and received, making literature more relatable and thought-provoking for its audience.

One key aspect of Realism was its emphasis on ordinary subjects. Unlike preceding literary movements that often highlighted extraordinary events or heroic figures, Realist authors turned their attention to the lives of ordinary people. This focus created reading experiences that resonated with many readers, allowing them to see themselves reflected in the narratives. For instance, instead of grand adventures or fantastical journeys, Realist novels might depict the daily struggles of working-class individuals, domestic life, or the complexities of small-town existence. By doing so, these stories challenged the notion that literature must only depict the exceptional, presenting the ordinary as worthy of exploration and reflection.

The emphasis on the mundane provided a fresh perspective on what constituted a compelling story. Readers found comfort and connection in seeing the everyday moments of their lives mirrored in the pages of a book. This relatability made the narratives feel more personal and underscored a universal human experience, bridging the gap between the author and the audience. Additionally, this approach democratised literature, suggesting that every individual's story has value and significance.

Social commentary became another defining feature of Realist novels. Authors used their works to critique societal norms and highlight injustices, prompting readers to engage in ethical and moral discussions. For example, books by Charles Dickens extensively portrayed the harsh realities of industrial society, exposing the plight of the poor and marginalised. Through characters like Oliver Twist or Hard Times' Stephen Blackpool, Dickens tells fascinating stories and encourages readers to reflect on social inequalities and consider the need for change. Similarly, George Eliot's Middlemarch delved into political reform, women's rights, and the limitations imposed by class and gender. These novels acted as mirrors to society, reflecting its flaws and urging readers to contemplate their roles within it.

This critical perspective invigorated literature with a sense of purpose beyond mere entertainment. Books became tools for social examination and progress, stirring public awareness and empathy towards pressing issues. Moreover, by embedding these critiques within engaging narratives, Realist authors ensured their messages reached a broad audience, making complex social topics accessible and understandable.

Attention to detail in setting and character descriptions is another hallmark of Realist literature. Authors fostered immersive narratives that captivated readers by meticulously crafting vivid scenes and lifelike characters. The rich details of a city's streets, the texture of an old farm, or the bustling atmosphere of a market square added depth to the stories. Gustave Flaubert's "Madame Bovary" is a prime example, where the meticulous depiction of Emma Bovary's provincial life enhances the narrative's realism and impact. Every nuance, from the furnishings in Emma's home to the expressions of minor characters, paints a comprehensive picture of her world, making it tangible for readers.

This meticulous attention to detail allowed readers to fully immerse themselves in the story's environment, experiencing the sights, sounds, and emotions just as the characters did. The authenticity of these settings contributed to the overall believability of the narrative, fostering a deeper emotional connection between the reader and the story. It also showcased the writer's skill in observation and description, elevating the craft of novel writing.

Complex characters form yet another pillar of Realist fiction. Unlike earlier literature's archetypal heroes and villains, Realist novels presented characters with multifaceted personalities, mirroring real human experiences. These characters were often deeply flawed, grappling with internal conflicts and external pressures that made their journeys unpredictable and relatable. For instance, in "Anna Karenina," Leo Tolstoy explores Anna's tumultuous emotions and moral dilemmas, painting a nuanced portrait of a woman torn between societal expectations and personal desires. Her complexity makes her both intriguing and empathetic, urging readers to look beyond superficial judgments and understand the factors influencing her actions.

Realist authors emphasised life's unpredictability and the diverse spectrum of human emotions by depicting characters with all their strengths, weaknesses, aspirations, and fears. This approach prompted readers to empathise with the characters, recognise the shared aspects of humanity, and reflect on their own lives and choices. It also underscored the idea that there are no simple answers or straightforward paths in life, encouraging a more compassionate and considerate view of others.

Realism's focus on ordinary subjects, social commentary, detailed settings, and complex characters collectively transformed the novel into a powerful medium for exploring and understanding the human condition. It broke away from romanticised and idealised portrayals, offering a more honest and grounded depiction of life. This authenticity resonated with readers, making literature a mirror to society and a tool for personal and collective reflection.

Prominent Authors and Their Contributions

Jane Austen's novels are fascinating examples of how Romanticism and Realism can intertwine. In her works, she masterfully combines elements of romance with a keen social observation. Take "Pride and Prejudice," for instance. The novel is often celebrated for its romantic storyline, with the evolving relationship between Elizabeth Bennet and Mr Darcy at its centre. Yet, Austen goes beyond mere romance, offering sharp insights into human relationships through her use of irony and wit. She carefully observes the societal norms and expectations of the early 19th century, highlighting issues such as class and marriage.

Austen's characters are vividly drawn and relatable, reflecting the everyday experiences of her time. Her heroines, in particular, are strong, intelligent women who navigate the constraints of their society with grace and determination. Austen provides readers with a nuanced view of human nature by focusing on these personal and social dynamics, making her novels timeless and relevant even today. Her blend of Romantic idealism with the stark realities of social life creates a rich narrative that continues to resonate with audiences.

Shifting gears, Charles Dickens is a monumental figure in 19th-century literature for portraying socioeconomic issues. His novels are a testament to the power of storytelling in drawing attention to social injustices. "Oliver Twist" is a prime example of Dickens' ability to bring to life the harsh realities of the poor and marginalised. Through his richly drawn characters, Dickens exposes the grim conditions of workhouses, the brutality of criminal underworlds, and the stark disparity between the wealthy and the impoverished.

Dickens' narrative technique often involves detailed descriptions and vivid imagery, which make the settings and characters leap off the page. This approach captivates readers and reinforces the social commentary inherent in his works. By humanising the struggles of his characters,

Dickens encourages empathy and social awareness among his readers, urging them to consider the implications of poverty and inequality in their society.

In contrast to Austen and Dickens, Emily Brontë's contribution to 19th-century literature is marked by her use of Gothic elements and complex characters. Her novel "Wuthering Heights" delves deep into human passions, exploring love, revenge, and madness themes. The story is set against the bleak, windswept moors, which serve as a fitting backdrop for the intense emotions experienced by the characters. Brontë's narrative structure is unconventional, employing multiple narrators and a non-linear timeline, which adds complexity to the story.

Brontë's characters, particularly Heathcliff and Catherine, are deeply flawed and driven by intense, often destructive passions. This focus on inner turmoil and emotional depth is a hallmark of Romantic literature. However, Brontë also infuses her narrative with elements of Realism, portraying the harsh consequences of the character's actions and the inevitable decay of Wuthering Heights itself. This interplay between Romantic idealism and realistic outcomes creates a powerful, haunting narrative that continues to captivate readers.

On the other hand, Gustave Flaubert's "Madame Bovary" is a cornerstone of literary Realism. Flaubert's meticulous attention to detail and his commitment to depicting life as it is sets his work apart. The novel tells the story of Emma Bovary, a woman whose romantic ideals clash with the mundane realities of provincial life. Flaubert's prose is precise and unembellished, mirroring everyday existence's ordinary, even trivial aspects. Through Emma's tragic pursuit of unattainable dreams, Flaubert critiques the notion of Romantic idealism.

Emma's dissatisfaction with her life and her relentless quest for something more reflect a broader commentary on the limitations and discontents of bourgeois society. Flaubert's realism lies in his unapologetic portrayal of human flaws and societal hypocrisies. He does not stop depicting life's banal and often bleak aspects, emphasising the contrast between romantic fantasies and real-life experiences. "Madame Bovary" thus serves as a poignant critique of romantic aspirations and a testament to the power of realist literature in revealing the truths of human existence.

These authors highlight the diverse approaches to Romanticism and Realism in 19th-century novels. Jane Austen's romance and social observation blend offers a witty yet insightful look into human relationships and societal norms. Charles Dickens' rich characterisations and focus on social issues bring to light the injustices faced by the lower classes. Emily Brontë's exploration of gothic themes and human passions challenges traditional narratives and structures. Meanwhile, Gustave Flaubert's commitment to realism provides a stark, objective critique of romantic ideals and the everyday struggles of ordinary life.

Social and Cultural Influences

The 19th century was an immense social and cultural change, profoundly influencing the themes and styles of novels written during this era. Exploring these contexts helps us understand how literature reflects and responds to the evolving world.

One significant driving force behind these changes was the Industrial Revolution. The rapid urbanisation and industrial growth led to notable shifts in society, which were vividly captured in the literature of the time. Authors like Charles Dickens delved into the harsh realities of urban life, highlighting class disparities and the struggles of the working class. Novels such as "Hard Times" and "Oliver Twist" offer readers a glimpse into the grim conditions of factories and slums, painting a stark picture of societal evolution. These stories did not merely entertain but served as social commentaries, urging readers to reflect on the implications of industrial progress and the accompanying human cost.

Another vital theme in 19th-century literature was the changing dynamics of gender roles and the rise of feminist thought. In a society predominately governed by patriarchal norms, novelists began to challenge traditional roles, offering new perspectives on women's lives and their quest for equality. Writers like Jane Austen and the Brontë sisters infused their narratives with strong, complex female characters who sought personal agency and defied conventional expectations. Austen's "Pride and Prejudice," for instance, not only critiques the institution of marriage but also promotes discussions about individual choice and empowerment. Such narratives opened up conversations about gender and laid the groundwork for later feminist movements, encouraging readers to re-evaluate the status quo and imagine a more equitable society.

Themes of imperialism and cultural identity brought about by colonialism also featured prominently in 19th-century novels. As European powers expanded their colonies, the resulting encounters with different cultures and the ensuing power dynamics were critically examined by contemporary writers. Works like Joseph Conrad's "Heart of Darkness" scrutinised the exploitative nature of imperialism and its dehumanising effects. This novel, albeit controversial, forces readers to confront the brutal realities of colonisation and question the moral justifications of empire-building. By weaving these global issues into their stories, authors encouraged readers to think deeply about cultural identity, history, and the far-reaching impacts of colonial rule.

The political landscape of the 19th century, marked by movements such as socialism and liberalism, also left an indelible imprint on literature. These ideologies often shaped narrative conflicts and provided a richer understanding of historical context. For example, Victor Hugo's "Les Misérables" is set against the backdrop of political upheaval in France, blending personal and political struggles to create a compelling narrative. Through the character of Jean Valjean and others, Hugo explores themes of justice, redemption, and the fight against oppression, mirroring the broader social currents of his time. Novels like these did more than tell individual stories; they captured the spirit of their age, offering insights into the complexities of political ideologies and their real-world consequences.

What We Learnt

In this chapter, we delved into the fascinating worlds of Realism and Romanticism, examining their profound impact on 19th-century novels. We explored how Romantic authors like Mary Shelley and Emily Brontë used emotionally charged narratives, nature symbolism, and elements of fantasy to evoke intense feelings and connect with readers on a personal level. In contrast, Realist writers like Charles Dickens focused on depicting everyday life, emphasising social issues, and creating richly detailed settings and complex characters mirrored real human experiences.

As we reflect on these literary movements' contrasting themes and techniques, it's clear that both Realism and Romanticism have significantly shaped the novel's evolution. Romanticism's focus on individuality, heroism, and the supernatural provided a means to explore deeper truths and human emotions. At the same time, Realism's attention to ordinary subjects, social commentary, and vivid details offered a grounded portrayal of life. Together, these approaches enriched literature by broadening its scope and enhancing readers' understanding of the human condition.

CHAPTER IV

Modernism and the Novel

"Modernism in the early 20th century brought a transformative shift to the world of literature, especially in the realm of the novel. Writers began experimenting with new narrative forms and techniques, breaking away from traditional storytelling methods. These innovative approaches sought to mirror modern life's chaotic and fragmented reality, challenging the conventions previously defining the genre."

This chapter will explore how Modernist authors revolutionised the novel by rejecting linear plots and conventional character development. We will explore their experimentation with form and style, examining the use of fragmented prose, unconventional punctuation, and other stylistic innovations. Additionally, we will look at the themes of ambiguity and uncertainty that pervade Modernist literature, emphasising the subjective nature of experience and truth. Through this exploration, readers will gain insight into the significant contributions of Modernist writers to the evolution of storytelling and their enduring impact on literature.

Break from traditional narrative forms.

The early 20th century marked a significant shift in the world of literature, especially with the advent of Modernism. Modernist authors sought to break away from traditional storytelling techniques and embrace new, innovative narrative strategies that better reflect modern life and thought's complexities and fragmented nature.

One of the most notable changes introduced by Modernist writers was the rejection of linear plots. Unlike their predecessors, favouring chronological and straightforward narratives, Modernist authors often employed non-linear storytelling methods. This approach was designed to challenge readers' expectations and encourage them to engage more deeply with the text. By presenting events out of sequence or through multiple perspectives, these authors created a sense of disorientation and reflection on how narratives could mirror the chaos and unpredictability of everyday life.

For instance, James Joyce's "Ulysses" is a seminal example of this technique. The novel does not follow a conventional plot structure but instead portrays a single day in the life of its protagonist through a series of episodes. Each episode employs different styles and techniques, reflecting the fragmented and multifaceted nature of the human experience. Similarly, Virginia Woolf's "Mrs. Dalloway" interweaves the thoughts and experiences of various characters within a single day, moving seamlessly between past and present, thereby dismantling the linear progression of time.

Another essential aspect of Modernist literature is the unconventional development of characters. Traditional novels often depicted well-defined, morally clear-cut characters. However, Modernist authors introduced characters who were far more ambiguous and internally conflicted, mirroring the uncertainties and complexities of modern life. These characters often grappled with existential questions, identity crises, and inner turmoil, providing a more profound psychological dimension to storytelling.

In "To the Lighthouse," Virginia Woolf creates introspective and multifaceted characters. The novel delves into its characters' inner lives, revealing their thoughts, emotions, and perceptions in a stream-of-consciousness style. This technique allows readers to explore the characters' subjectivities and understand their motivations beyond surface-level actions and dialogue.

Modernist writers also experimented with form and style, pushing the boundaries of traditional prose. Fragmented prose, unconventional punctuation, and innovative narrative structures became hallmarks of Modernist literature. These stylistic choices aimed to capture the fragmented reality of modern life, making the reading experience more immersive and reflective of the chaotic world outside the text.

One standout example of experimental style is found in Gertrude Stein's works. Her prose often defies conventional grammar and syntax, creating a rhythm and flow that challenges readers to reconsider their expectations of language and meaning. This experimentation with language highlights the fluidity and subjectivity of human perception, encouraging readers to engage with the text on a deeper level.

Ambiguity and uncertainty are recurring themes in Modernist literature, emphasising the subjective nature of experience and the elusiveness of absolute truth. Modernist authors often left their narratives open-ended, inviting readers to draw conclusions and interpretations. This emphasis on ambiguity reflects the time's broader cultural and philosophical shifts as people grappled with the uncertainties of a rapidly changing world.

T.S. Eliot's poem "The Waste Land" epitomises the theme of ambiguity in Modernist literature. The poem is fragmented and filled with obscure references, creating a sense of dislocation and confusion. Eliot's use of multiple voices and shifting perspectives further underscores the idea that meaning is not fixed but constructed by individual interpretation. This ambiguity forces readers to engage with the text actively, piecing together its meaning based on their experiences and understanding.

Through these innovative techniques and themes, Modernist authors reshaped the landscape of literature, challenging traditional conventions and encouraging readers to embrace new ways of thinking. Their rejection of linear plots, unconventional character development, experimental styles, and emphasis on ambiguity and uncertainty reflect the complexities and contradictions of modern life. As we delve deeper into Modernist writers' works, we gain a greater appreciation for their contributions to the evolution of storytelling and their enduring impact on literature.

By breaking away from established norms, Modernist authors not only mirrored the fragmented reality of the 20th century but also paved the way for future literary movements to explore new forms of expression. Their willingness to experiment and push boundaries inspires writers and readers alike, reminding us of the ever-evolving nature of literature and its ability to capture the essence of the human experience.

Stream of consciousness technique

The stream-of-consciousness technique is a hallmark of Modernist literature, representing a radical departure from traditional narrative forms. By diving into the inner workings of characters' minds, authors like Virginia Woolf and James Joyce sought to capture the multifaceted nature of human thought and perception.

At its core, the stream-of-consciousness technique involves a continuous flow of thoughts, feelings, and experiences that pass through a character's mind. This method allows readers to experience the character's mental landscape directly, often without the mediation of an external, objective narrator. Unlike conventional storytelling, which tends to follow a structured sequence of events, the stream of consciousness can appear fragmented and disjointed, mirroring the real-life complexity of human cognition.

Virginia Woolf masterfully employs this technique in "Mrs. Dalloway" and "To the Lighthouse." In "Mrs. Dalloway," Woolf navigates between the minds of various characters, revealing their innermost thoughts and emotions in a way that feels immediate and intimate. For instance, as Clarissa Dalloway prepares for her party, her thoughts flow seamlessly between past and present, touching on memories, sensory impressions, and fleeting reflections. This approach deepens our understanding of Clarissa and creates a rich tapestry of interconnected consciousnesses that define the novel.

James Joyce takes the stream of consciousness to new heights in "Ulysses," where he delves deep into the minds of his characters, notably Leopold Bloom and Stephen Dedalus. Joyce's style in "Ulysses" is dense and innovative, blending inner monologues with many literary techniques to reflect thoughts' chaotic and overlapping nature. One of the most compelling sections is Molly Bloom's soliloquy at the novel's end, where her unfiltered thoughts reveal the full spectrum of her emotions and desires. Here, the stream of consciousness dissolves the boundary between the character's mind and the reader, offering unparalleled access to her internal world.

This technique significantly impacts character development by providing a nuanced portrayal of a character's psychology. Traditional narratives often rely on dialogue and action to convey character traits and motivations. However, the stream of consciousness goes beyond surface-level interactions, delving into the underlying thoughts and feelings that shape a character's behaviour. Through this method, readers gain insight into the complexities and contradictions of characters, making them more realistic and relatable.

For example, in Woolf's "To the Lighthouse," the character of Mrs. Ramsay is explored through her fleeting thoughts and perceptions. Her moments of introspection reveal her concerns about family, beauty, and the passage of time, painting a detailed picture of her inner life. Such a deep dive into mental processes makes Mrs. Ramsay more than just a figure in a story; she becomes a fully realised individual whose subjective experiences resonate with readers on a personal level.

Moreover, the influence of the stream of consciousness on modern literature cannot be overstated. This technique has set a precedent for subsequent literary movements, paving the way for writers to explore new narrative possibilities. The direct engagement with a character's mind has inspired many authors to experiment with the boundaries of storytelling, resulting in a diverse range of stylistic innovations.

In contemporary literature, the legacy of the stream of consciousness can be seen in the works of authors like Toni Morrison and Haruki Murakami. In novels such as Beloved, Morrison uses a similar approach to delve into her characters' traumatic memories and emotional depths, creating a powerful and immersive reading experience. On the other hand, Murakami blends realism with surreal elements, often using internal monologues to blur the lines between reality and imagination.

The enduring appeal of this technique lies in its ability to capture the authentic, intricate nature of human thought. Readers are drawn to the immediacy and intimacy it provides, allowing them to connect with characters on a deeper emotional level. As a result, the stream of consciousness continues to be a vital tool for writers seeking to explore the complexities of the human psyche.

Understanding the stream-of-consciousness technique enriches our appreciation of Modernist literature and its contributions to the evolution of the novel. By breaking free from the constraints of traditional narrative forms, Modernist authors have opened up new avenues for storytelling, emphasising the fluid and dynamic nature of human consciousness. This shift reflects the broader cultural and intellectual currents of the early 20th century and resonates with contemporary readers who seek to understand individuals' multifaceted experiences.

Focus on inner psychology.

In the early 20th century, Modernist authors shifted the landscape of novel writing by emphasising inner psychology and subjective experience. These authors sought to break away from traditional storytelling techniques, examining the depths of human consciousness and how it shapes our understanding of the world.

One of the hallmarks of Modernist literature is psychological realism. Unlike previous literary movements, which often focused on external events and actions, Modernism delves into the complexities of the human mind. Authors such as Virginia Woolf, James Joyce, and Marcel Proust explored characters' innermost thoughts, feelings, and motivations. This approach offered readers a more intimate and nuanced portrayal of characters, making their experiences feel authentic and profound.

For instance, in Virginia Woolf's "Mrs. Dalloway," we see the protagonist navigating her day while simultaneously experiencing a tumultuous inner life filled with memories, doubts, and aspirations. Woolf's narrative technique allows readers to enter the character's stream of consciousness, providing a layered understanding of her personality. This depth of psychological exploration became a defining feature of Modernist novels, setting them apart from their predecessors.

Symbolism also plays a critical role in conveying inner psychology within Modernist literature. Authors often used symbolic imagery to represent complex emotional and mental states, enriching the narrative. For example, in James Joyce's "A Portrait of the Artist as a Young Man," the bird imagery and references to flight symbolise the protagonist's yearning for artistic and personal freedom. Using symbols, Modernist writers could communicate abstract concepts and emotions more vividly than straightforward descriptions alone.

To effectively analyse symbolism in Modernist literature, consider the following steps:

1. Identify recurring symbols or images within the text.
2. Reflect on what these symbols might represent regarding the characters' inner lives.
3. Examine how these symbols interact with the novel's broader themes.

Readers can gain deeper insights into the portrayed psychological landscapes by paying close attention to symbolic elements.

Memory and perception are integral to the Modernist exploration of identity. In "In Search of Lost Time," authors like Marcel Proust intricately weaves the past and present, showing how memories shape one's sense of self and reality. Proust famously illustrates this through the taste of a madeleine cake, which triggers an involuntary flood of childhood memories for the narrator. This emphasis on memory underscores the belief that our identities are not fixed but constantly evolving based on our recollections and interpretations of past experiences.

Moreover, perception plays a significant role in how characters understand their world. In "To the Lighthouse," Virginia Woolf presents different perspectives of the same events through various characters' eyes, highlighting the subjectivity of experience. This approach demonstrates that reality is not a single objective truth but a mosaic of individual perceptions and memories.

When analysing the role of memory and perception in Modernist texts, it is helpful to ask:

1. How do characters' memories influence their actions and decisions?
2. In what ways do different characters perceive the same events or situations differently?
3. What does this reveal about the nature of truth and reality within the novel?

Such questions can help uncover the layers of meaning that Modernist authors embedded in their narratives.

Emphasising subjective truth is another cornerstone of Modernist literature. Writers during this period were keenly aware that truth is multifaceted and deeply personal. They challenged the notion of an absolute, universal truth, suggesting that each constructs their version of reality based on personal experiences and perceptions.

In T.S. Eliot's poem "The Love Song of J. Alfred Prufrock," the protagonist grapples with his insecurities and the fragmented nature of his existence. The poem's disjointed structure and stream-of-consciousness style reflect the complexity of Prufrock's internal world, emphasising that his truth is subjective and diverse.

Subjective truth invites readers to engage with texts more actively and interpretively. It encourages them to consider multiple viewpoints and acknowledge the limitations of any single perspective. This openness to ambiguity and various interpretations became a defining feature of Modernist works, inviting readers to delve deeper into the text and discover their meanings.

Prominent modernist authors and texts

The early 20th century marked a significant shift in literature, characterised by the rise of Modernism. This subpoint focuses on key modernist authors and their pioneering works, providing insight into the diversity of approaches within the movement.

One of the most influential figures in modernist literature is Virginia Woolf. Her novels, "Mrs. Dalloway" and "To the Lighthouse," exemplify her innovative narrative techniques. In "Mrs. Dalloway," Woolf delves into the inner lives of her characters through a stream-of-consciousness style, presenting an intricate tapestry of thoughts and memories. She breaks away from linear storytelling, opting for a fragmented narrative that mirrors the complexity of human consciousness. The novel unfolds over a single day yet captures life's emotions and experiences. Similarly, in "To the Lighthouse," Woolf explores time and existential reflection themes. The novel oscillates between different characters' perspectives, offering a multifaceted view of reality. Through these works, Woolf challenges traditional narrative structures, highlighting the fluidity and subjectivity of human experience.

James Joyce stands as another pillar of modernist literature, with his seminal work, "Ulysses," often hailed as a masterpiece of the movement. "Ulysses" redefines the boundaries of the novel, employing an array of styles and techniques that were revolutionary for its time. The novel chronicles a single day in the life of Leopold Bloom, but its scope encompasses profound explorations of identity, memory, and perception. Joyce's use of stream-of-consciousness, along with his rich allusions to classical mythology and literature, creates a dense, intertextual fabric. Each chapter presents a distinct narrative style, ranging from interior monologue to newspaper headlines, underscoring the fragmented nature of modern existence. "Ulysses" challenges readers to engage deeply with its text, reflecting the complexities and dissonances of contemporary life.

Franz Kafka starkly contrasts his unique brand of modernism, emphasising themes of alienation and existential dread. Kafka's novella, "The Metamorphosis," captures the unsettling transformation of Gregor Samsa into a gigantic insect. This bizarre occurrence is a powerful metaphor for the alienation and dehumanisation experienced by individuals in modern society. Kafka's prose is straightforward yet evocative, creating a sense of unease that permeates the narrative. The novella delves into Gregor's psyche, examining his isolation from family and society. Kafka's work often blurs the line between reality and nightmare, portraying a world where incomprehensible and impersonal forces trap individuals. His ability to tap into universal anxieties makes "The Metamorphosis" a cornerstone of modernist literature, resonating with readers across generations.

T.S. Eliot's contributions to modernist literature, mainly through poetry, further illustrate the movement's diversity. "The Waste Land," one of Eliot's most renowned works, epitomises modernist themes of fragmentation and despair. Composed of five sections, the poem weaves many voices, languages, and literary references, creating a collage of modern life. "The Waste Land" reflects the disintegration of cultural and spiritual certainties in the aftermath of World War I. Eliot employs a range of poetic forms and techniques, including free verse, dramatic monologue, and pastiche, to convey contemporary existence's chaotic and disjointed nature. His use of mythological and religious allusions provides a framework through which he interrogates modernity, searching for meaning in a fractured world. Eliot's innovative style and profound thematic exploration make his work vital to modernist literature.

Each author—Woolf, Joyce, Kafka, and Eliot—brings a distinct voice and approach to the modernist movement. Their works challenge conventional narratives, inviting readers to reconsider the nature of reality and experience. They capture the essence of modern life's complexity and ambiguity through experimentation with form, language, and perspective. By studying their contributions, readers understand how modernist literature reflects and responds to the tumultuous changes of the early 20th century.

What we Learnt

As we draw this chapter to a close, we've seen how Modernist authors in the early 20th century revolutionised storytelling by stepping away from traditional linear narratives. These writers, including Virginia Woolf and James Joyce, embraced non-linear plots and multiple perspectives to reflect the fragmented nature of modern life. Their techniques challenged readers to engage more deeply with their texts, creating a rich tapestry of disorientation and reflection mirrored everyday experiences' unpredictability. Through experimental styles, unconventional character development, and ambiguous endings, Modernist authors offered a new lens through which to view the complexities and contradictions of human existence.

The impact of these innovations extends beyond just the pages of their books. By breaking established norms, Modernist writers paved the way for future literary movements to explore newer forms of expression. Their willingness to push boundaries inspires writers and readers today, reminding us of literature's ever-evolving nature and its power to capture the multifaceted essence of human life. Through their enduring works, Modernist authors not only encapsulated the spirit of their time but also left a lasting legacy on the world of literature.

CHAPTER V

Postmodernism and Beyond

"Exploring postmodern novels is a fascinating journey into fragmented narratives and paradoxes that defy traditional storytelling conventions. These works often reflect the chaotic nature of modern life through disjointed plots and characters who embody conflicting traits. By breaking away from linear progression, postmodern literature presents a mosaic of experiences, urging readers to embrace the unpredictability of existence. Whether it's a character becoming "unstuck in time" or grappling with an unresolved conspiracy, these stories mirror the complexities and uncertainties we face in reality."

This chapter will delve into the innovative techniques that define postmodern novels and set them apart from earlier literary movements. Expect to uncover how authors construct their narratives using fragmentation, cyclic structures, and intertextuality. We'll also explore metaphysical themes and instances where authors break the fourth wall, drawing attention to the act of writing itself. As we navigate through these diverse techniques, you'll see how postmodern literature invites readers to actively participate in creating meaning, redefining our relationship with fiction.

Fragmentation and Paradox

Postmodern novels often disrupt conventional storytelling methods, presenting fragmented narratives that mirror the chaotic nature of contemporary life. This narrative disjunction breaks from linear progression, offering a mosaic of experiences and perspectives. For instance, in Kurt Vonnegut's "Slaughterhouse-Five," the protagonist, Billy Pilgrim, becomes "unstuck in time," resulting in a story that jumps across different periods of his life. This technique emphasises life's unpredictability, reflecting how people might not experience events in a neat, sequential order.

In postmodern literature, contradictions are common as well. Characters and plots may embody conflicting traits or situations that highlight uncertainty and complexity. A vivid example is Thomas Pynchon's "The Crying of Lot 49," where the protagonist, Oedipa Maas, grapples with an intricate conspiracy that never fully resolves. The novel leaves readers questioning what is real and imagined, underscoring the theme of ambiguity. Similarly, Don DeLillo's "White Noise" features characters who exhibit contradictory behaviours, such as simultaneously fearing and longing for death. These contradictions force readers to confront their assumptions and acknowledge the multifaceted nature of reality.

Cyclic structures also play a significant role in postmodern narratives. Many stories revisit earlier plot points or themes but with altered meanings. This cyclical approach can be seen in Gabriel Garcia Marquez's "One Hundred Years of Solitude," where the Buendía family's history repeats itself through generations, incorporating new interpretations with each cycle. The sense of certainty in the characters' lives reflects a broader commentary on human nature and societal patterns. The cyclical structure invites readers to recognise recurring motifs and question whether progress or change is possible.

Intertextuality is another crucial element of postmodernism, as it enriches narratives by referencing and alluding to other texts. This technique creates layers of meaning, enhancing the complexity of the story. For instance, in Michael Cunningham's "The Hours," the narrative weaves together the lives of three women connected by Virginia Woolf's "Mrs. Dalloway." By drawing from Woolf's work, Cunningham adds depth to his characters' experiences and emphasises the enduring influence of literature. Such intertextual references encourage readers to explore connections between different works and appreciate how stories can inform and transform one another.

Metafiction and Self-referentiality

Metafiction is a crucial characteristic of postmodern novels, representing a fascinating shift from traditional storytelling methods. In postmodern literature, authors frequently use techniques that draw attention to the act of writing. One such method is an authorial intrusion, where the author directly addresses readers or inserts themselves into the narrative. This breaks the fourth wall and invites readers to think about the nature of fiction and reality within the novel. For instance, in Kurt Vonnegut's "Breakfast of Champions," Vonnegut not only narrates but also becomes a character in his own story, engaging with his creations and making the reader acutely aware of the artificiality of the narrative.

Another hallmark of metafiction in postmodern novels is varied narrative techniques that disrupt the conventional flow of storytelling. Authors may employ footnotes, commentary, and unconventional formats to create interruptions and layers within the text. These techniques remind readers that they are engaging with a constructed work. For example, in David Foster Wallace's "Infinite Jest," extensive and detailed footnotes provide additional context, alternative perspectives, and even entire subplots, creating a multi-dimensional reading experience that challenges traditional linear narratives. By doing so, Wallace adds depth to the story and demands active engagement from the reader, who must navigate between the main text and the footnotes.

Additionally, postmodern authors often explore simultaneous realities by presenting multiple narratives or endings. This approach questions the notion of a singular absolute truth and reflects the complexities and ambiguities of modern life. In Italo Calvino's "If on a Winter's Night a Traveler," the novel consists of several different stories, each introduced as if it were the beginning of a new book. The fragmented structure invites readers to consider the relationship between the various narratives and challenges them to piece together an understanding from seemingly unrelated fragments. This technique not only highlights the artificial nature of storytelling but also emphasises the interpretative role of the reader in constructing meaning.

Playfulness is another common feature in metafictional works, where authors incorporate humour and irony to engage with literary tropes lightheartedly. This playfulness can serve to both entertain and critique traditional narrative forms. An example of this can be seen in John Barth's "Lost in the Funhouse," where the story is filled with self-referential humour and addresses the struggles of creating fiction. Barth's playful style underscores the contrived elements of storytelling and the challenges writers face while simultaneously entertaining the reader with its wit and cleverness.

One practical guideline when analysing postmodern novels is to identify instances of these narrative techniques. When you come across direct authorial intrusion, note how it alters your perception of the story and the author's relationship with the text. For narrative techniques like footnotes or commentary, consider how these elements add complexity to the narrative and influence your reading experience. When encountering simultaneous realities, reflect on how different narratives might intersect or diverge and what this says about the nature of truth in the novel. Observing playfulness and paying attention to how humour and irony are used to critique literary conventions can also provide valuable insights.

In postmodern literature, the breaking down of traditional narrative boundaries invites readers to become more aware of the constructed nature of stories. This awareness is crucial for understanding the broader themes and innovations of postmodernism. By engaging with techniques such as authorial intrusion, unconventional narrative formats, simultaneous realities, and playful commentary, readers gain a deeper appreciation for the complexities and nuances of postmodern novels. These techniques challenge conventional storytelling and encourage readers to actively participate in creating meaning, transforming the reading experience into a dynamic and interactive process.

Blurring of Genres and Styles

When it comes to understanding postmodern novels, one of the most intriguing aspects is how they defy traditional genre boundaries. This subpoint delves into the innovative ways these works blur the lines between genres, creating unique and multifaceted narratives.

Postmodern novels are renowned for their genre hybridity. Unlike conventional literature that typically adheres to a defined genre—be it romance, horror, or mystery—postmodern works often mix elements from various genres. Imagine a narrative that seamlessly combines fantasy, science fiction, and realism. These eclectic combinations produce more prosperous and complex stories, pushing readers to engage with the text on multiple levels. One minute, a character may be navigating a dystopian future; the next, they're plunged into a mythic past complete with fantastical creatures.

One well-known example of genre hybridity is Margaret Atwood's "The Handmaid's Tale." This novel blends dystopian fiction with feminist critique, speculative fiction, and even elements of historical fiction. The diversity of genres within a single work challenges readers to think beyond the confines of traditional literary categories. Another landmark piece is Thomas Pynchon's "Gravity's Rainbow," which merges elements of historical fiction, science fiction, and political satire. Through these examples, it becomes evident that postmodern authors delight in experimenting with genre, crafting stories as unpredictable as they are engaging.

However, such innovation does not come without its complexities. The fluidity of form in postmodern literature can lead to ambiguity in classification. Many texts resist straightforward categorisation, challenging readers to reconsider their relationships with familiar genres. Take, for instance, Haruki Murakami's "Kafka on the Shore." This novel defies easy classification—it is part of magical realism, mystery, and philosophical quest. Such ambiguity forces us to question what defines a genre and encourages a deeper exploration of the themes and motifs within the story.

Adding another layer of complexity, postmodern authors often re-invent familiar tropes to satirical or critical ends. Tropes are recurring themes or clichés commonly found within specific genres. In the hands of a postmodernist, these tropes are turned on their heads and used to both acknowledge and subvert traditional storytelling techniques. For example, Kurt Vonnegut's "Slaughterhouse-Five" employs the time travel trope. Still, instead of using it for straightforward adventure, Vonnegut uses it to explore the trauma of war and the fragmented nature of human experience. This reworking critiques traditional narratives and offers fresh insights into well-worn themes.

Opening up the dialogue further, let's consider the role of satire in repurposing genre tropes. Joseph Heller's "Catch-22" takes the war novel—a genre traditionally laden with heroism and patriotism—and turns it into a darkly humorous critique of bureaucratic absurdity and the futility of war. By employing irony and exaggeration, Heller deconstructs the heroic archetypes typically found in war stories, presenting a far more chaotic and cynical view of conflict. This satirical approach compels readers to question previously held beliefs about war and heroism, urging them to adopt a more critical perspective.

Given the mutable nature of postmodern literature, guidelines for understanding genre hybridity are essential for readers looking to navigate these complex works successfully. To fully appreciate postmodern novels, one should approach the text with an open mind and be ready to accept unconventional narrative techniques. First, it's crucial to recognise and embrace the blending of genres without categorising the work immediately. Instead of trying to fit the novel into a predefined box, let the story unfold naturally, revealing its unique structure and thematic depth.

Second, pay attention to how familiar tropes are used and reinvented. Recognising these modifications can provide insight into the author's intent and the broader commentary. Whether through satire, irony, or parody, these reworked tropes serve as a lens through which the reader can critically analyse the narrative. Finally, accept ambiguity as a feature rather than a flaw. Postmodern novels often leave questions unanswered or present multiple interpretations, reflecting the complexity of contemporary life. Embracing this uncertainty can enhance one's appreciation of the narrative's richness and the author's creative vision.

Prominent Postmodern Novelists

Thomas Pynchon is a towering figure in postmodern literature. His novels are renowned for their complexity and thematic depth, often weaving together intricate plots that challenge the reader to pay close attention. Pynchon's works delve into themes of paranoia and conspiracy, creating a sense of uncertainty and intrigue. Novels like "Gravity's Rainbow" and "The Crying of Lot 49" artfully depict societies rife with hidden agendas and unseen forces shaping events from behind the scenes. These stories compel readers to question reality and consider the pervasive impact of secretive organisations and covert operations on our lives.

Don DeLillo is another significant author who has contributed substantially to postmodern literature. Known for his sharp insights into the media-saturated nature of contemporary society, DeLillo examines how communication and technology shape human perception and relationships. In his novel "White Noise," he explores how the constant barrage of media messages affects individuals' understanding of the world. DeLillo's work often presents a fragmented reality where characters struggle to find genuine connections amidst consumerism and mass media noise. This exploration of modern anxieties reflects broader postmodern concerns about authenticity and meaning in an increasingly mediated world.

Kurt Vonnegut stands out with his distinctive dark humour and satirical style. His novels blend fictional elements with pointed social critiques, making readers laugh while prompting them to think critically about societal issues. For example, "Slaughterhouse-Five" combines science fiction with a harrowing account of the bombing of Dresden during World War II, revealing the absurdity and tragedy of war. Vonnegut's use of humour allows him to address serious topics in a way that is both accessible and thought-provoking. His ability to mix genres and employ unconventional narrative techniques exemplifies the innovative spirit of postmodern literature.

Salman Rushdie brings a unique voice to postmodern literature by fusing magical realism with historical and political commentary. His novels often emphasise themes of cultural hybridity, reflecting his diverse heritage and experiences. In "Midnight's Children," Rushdie intertwines the personal story of a boy born during India's independence with the larger narrative of the nation's turbulent history. This blending of personal and political narratives challenges traditional storytelling conventions and highlights the interconnectedness of individual and collective identities. Rushdie's incorporation of fantastical elements deepens the reader's engagement with real-world issues, illustrating the power of storytelling to explore complex truths.

Through their unique styles and thematic preoccupations, these authors contribute to the rich tapestry of postmodern literature. Their works push the boundaries of traditional literary forms, inviting readers to question established norms and explore new ways of understanding the world. By examining the contributions of Pynchon, DeLillo, Vonnegut, and Rushdie, we gain a deeper appreciation for the diversity and innovation that characterise the postmodern literary movement. These authors entertain and provoke thought and reflection, encouraging readers to engage more deeply with the texts and their broader cultural contexts.

As we continue to study postmodern literature, it becomes clear that these authors have left an indelible mark on the literary landscape. Their willingness to experiment with form and content has opened up new possibilities for storytelling, allowing subsequent generations of writers to build on their pioneering efforts. Students and readers can better appreciate the complexities and nuances of postmodern novels by understanding the key themes and techniques employed by Pynchon, DeLillo, Vonnegut, and Rushdie. This deeper understanding enriches our reading experience and enhances our ability to engage critically with the texts.

What We Learnt

As we wrap up this chapter, we've delved into the fascinating world of postmodern novels. We explored how these works break away from traditional storytelling through fragmented narratives, paradoxes, and cyclic structures. Through examples like "Slaughterhouse-Five" and "The Crying of Lot 49," we saw how postmodern authors highlight life's unpredictability and ambiguity. Additionally, intertextuality enriches these stories by connecting them with other texts, allowing readers to uncover deeper meanings and connections.

We've also examined metafiction and its techniques, such as authorial intrusion and varied narrative methods. These elements invite readers to reflect on the nature of fiction and reality. By using unconventional formats and multiple narratives, as seen in "Infinite Jest" and "If on a Winter's Night a Traveler," postmodern authors challenge us to engage with their stories actively. This exploration reveals the playful yet critical spirit of postmodern literature, encouraging an interactive reading experience that makes us question our assumptions and embrace the complexities of contemporary life.

CHAPTER VI

Plot Structure

"Crafting a compelling narrative relies heavily on understanding plot structure. Every plot element works together, like puzzle pieces, to create a cohesive and engaging story that keeps readers hooked from beginning to end. Whether you're an aspiring writer or an avid reader looking to deepen your appreciation for literature, getting to grips with how plot structure operates is essential."

In this chapter, we will dissect the different components that makeup plot structure in novels. We'll begin by exploring exposition and the inciting incident, which set the stage and kickstarted the main action. Then, we move into rising action and conflict, where tension escalates, and characters face increasingly complex challenges. As we reach the climax, we'll examine how the story's peak moment of tension defines character arcs and drives the narrative forward. Finally, we'll delve into falling action and resolution, discussing how these elements tie up loose ends and provide satisfying closure. By the end of this chapter, you'll clearly understand how each plot piece contributes to crafting a narrative that captivates and engages its audience.

Exposition and Inciting Incident

In any novel, exposition is a critical element that sets the stage for everything to come. In these early pages, the author introduces us to the characters, establishes the setting, and provides the initial situation of the story. This foundation of background information is essential as it helps readers understand the context in which the narrative unfolds. By clearly defining the protagonist, supporting characters, and the world they inhabit, the exposition allows readers to become invested in the story from the outset.

Consider how J.K. Rowling masterfully sets up the world of Harry Potter in "Harry Potter and the Sorcerer's Stone." The first few chapters introduce Harry's mundane life with the Dursleys, his sense of being different, and the mysterious letters that begin arriving. These elements create a backdrop that piques the reader's curiosity about what lies ahead.

Once the stage is set, it becomes crucial to introduce the inciting incident, the catalyst that sets the main plot into motion. This event disrupts the initial situation and propels the protagonist into the story's central action. The inciting incident can take many forms—a letter, a meeting, an unexpected event—but its primary role is always to shake things up and challenge the status quo.

For example, in Suzanne Collins's "The Hunger Games," the reaping ceremony is the inciting incident. Katniss Everdeen's sister, Prim, is selected to participate in the deadly games, and Katniss volunteers to take her place. This moment completely alters the course of Katniss's life and plunges her into the heart of the conflict. The stakes are immediately raised, and readers are drawn into the tension and urgency of the narrative.

A well-crafted inciting incident initiates the central conflict and engages readers by creating a sense of anticipation and excitement. It provides an apparent reason for why the story must unfold and what the protagonist is up against. This aspect is crucial for maintaining reader interest and establishing the narrative's tone.

Another example is Harper Lee's To Kill a Mockingbird, which further illustrates the importance of the exposition and inciting incident. The exposition introduces us to Scout Finch, her brother Jem, and their father Atticus, who live in the racially tense town of Maycomb, Alabama. This setup is essential for understanding the social dynamics and the challenges the characters will face.

The inciting incident occurs when Atticus takes on the case of defending Tom Robinson, a Black man falsely accused of raping a white woman. This decision disrupts the initial state of equilibrium and thrusts the Finch family into the centre of the town's prejudice and moral battles. The resulting conflict drives the plot forward and deepens the reader's engagement with the themes of justice and inequality.

In addition to building engagement, a well-crafted exposition and inciting incident lay the groundwork for the story's emotional and thematic development. They establish the tone, whether it's the whimsical magic of Rowling's wizarding world or the grim realism of Collins' dystopian society. These elements draw readers in, making them care about the characters and their journeys.

Take, for instance, Jane Austen's "Pride and Prejudice." The exposition introduces us to the Bennet family, their social standing, and the pressures of marriage in Regency England. The arrival of Mr. Bingley and Mr. Darcy serves as the inciting incident that disrupts the family's routine and creates the central conflicts of love, class, and misunderstandings. This careful setup ensures readers are emotionally invested in Elizabeth Bennet's interactions and growth throughout the story.

Examining these examples shows how crucial the exposition and inciting incident are in crafting a compelling narrative. They provide the necessary background, launch the plot into motion, and hook readers by creating intrigue and anticipation. Without these foundational elements, a story risks falling flat, leaving readers disengaged and uninterested.

For aspiring writers and literature students alike, understanding the roles of exposition and inciting incidents can significantly enhance one's ability to analyse and appreciate novels. Recognising how an author sets the stage and propels the plot forward allows for a deeper appreciation of storytelling techniques and structure.

Moreover, English teachers and educators can utilise these concepts to help students connect more profoundly with the material. By breaking down the components of plot structure and analysing their impact, teachers can foster a more engaging and insightful classroom discussion. The ability to identify and discuss these elements not only improves literary analysis skills but also enhances students' overall enjoyment of reading.

Rising Action and Conflict

Rising action is a crucial component in any narrative structure. The backbone leads to the climax, the peak moment of tension and action in the story. The goal is to examine how rising action builds tension and develops conflict, which is essential for maintaining reader interest.

Understanding Rising Action is fundamental when dissecting a plot. Rising action comprises events that create suspense, complicate the plot, build stakes, and set the climax. These events are designed to engage the reader by incrementally increasing the characters' tension and complications. Each event should be more intense or complex than the last, leading the reader on an emotional journey that keeps them glued to the page. For instance, in J.K. Rowling's Harry Potter series, each book features escalating challenges that Harry must face, such as deciphering riddles or battling dark forces. These incremental tensions keep readers engaged and set the stage for the climactic battles at the end of each book.

Types of Conflict play a significant role in shaping the rising action. Both internal and external conflicts are vital here. Internal conflict involves the psychological struggles within a character. This could be doubts, fears, or moral dilemmas that add depth to their personality and make them more relatable. For example, in Fyodor Dostoevsky's "Crime and Punishment," Raskolnikov's internal conflict about morality and justice drives much of the rising action. On the other hand, external conflict involves characters facing outside forces, such as different characters, nature, society, or even technology. William Golding's "Lord of the Flies" illustrates external conflict through the characters' struggle for survival and order while stranded on an island. These conflicts propel the narrative forward by creating obstacles and challenges that need resolution, thereby keeping the reader invested.

Pacing and tension are vital in ensuring the rising action remains engaging without losing momentum. Proper pacing is about finding a balance where the story moves neither quickly nor slowly. If the increasing action is too fast-paced, it may overwhelm the reader, making it difficult to follow the storyline. Conversely, if it's too slow, the reader might lose interest. Pacing can be effectively managed by alternating between high-tension moments and calmer scenes. For example, Suzanne Collins's "The Hunger Games" balances intense action sequences with quieter, introspective moments that explore Katniss Everdeen's thoughts and feelings. This alternation keeps the reader engaged, offering breathers that prevent the narrative from becoming monotonous while maintaining overall tension.

Techniques for Creating Tension can vary widely among authors, but some standard methods include character dilemmas, escalating stakes, and foreshadowing. Character dilemmas involve difficult choices that force characters to reveal their true selves. These decisions often have significant consequences, adding complexity to the plot. For instance, George R.R. Martin's "A Song of Ice and Fire" series frequently places characters in morally ambiguous situations where they must choose between loyalty and survival, love and duty. Such dilemmas heighten engagement by making readers ponder what they would do in the same situation.

Escalating stakes means that the consequences of failure become progressively worse as the story unfolds. Initially, the stakes might involve personal losses or small-scale conflicts, but as the rising action progresses, these stakes escalate to life-or-death situations or large-scale disasters. In J.R.R. Tolkien's "The Lord of the Rings," the stakes rise from Frodo's safety to the fate of Middle-earth. This escalation keeps the reader invested by continually raising the level of threat and urgency.

Foreshadowing is another powerful technique for creating tension. Authors can build anticipation and keep readers guessing about future events by planting subtle hints or clues early in the narrative. Agatha Christie masterfully uses foreshadowing in her detective novels to drop clues that seem insignificant until the grand reveal. This method ensures that readers remain actively engaged, piecing together information and speculating about potential outcomes.

Climax and Turning Points

Understanding the climax is crucial when analysing plot structure, as it represents the pinnacle of the story's tension and conflict. The climax is where everything comes to a head; the protagonist faces their most significant challenge, and the trajectory of the narrative changes. It's the most intense part of the story, resolving major conflicts and testing characters in ways that demand decisive action. When readers reach this point, they often encounter heightened emotions and pivotal moments that define the rest of the story.

In many ways, the climax serves as the story's turning point. At this juncture, significant choices made by the protagonists or antagonists have lasting consequences. These choices clarify character arcs, revealing who the characters are under pressure. They also explore themes such as fate, free will, and agency, questioning whether characters are masters of their destinies or pawns of circumstance. For example, in J.K. Rowling's "Harry Potter and the Deathly Hallows," Harry's choice to face Voldemort alone in the Forbidden Forest is a defining moment that highlights his bravery and selflessness, ultimately shaping his character arc and the narrative outcome.

Examining notable climaxes across various genres can offer deeper insight into how different stories handle these critical moments. In Harper Lee's "To Kill a Mockingbird," the climax occurs during Tom Robinson's trial, where Atticus Finch presents his defence against deep-seated racial prejudices. This scene is intense and emotionally charged, testing not only Atticus but also the moral fibres of the community. In contrast, Suzanne Collins's "The

Hunger Games" climax is more action-oriented, featuring Katniss's decision to defy the Capitol by threatening a double suicide with Peeta. This act of rebellion significantly impacts the narrative arc and sets the stage for the subsequent books in the series.

Climaxes also vary in presentation depending on the genre. In romance novels, the climax might be an emotional confession or a grand romantic gesture, bringing characters closer after a conflict. In mystery or thriller genres, the climax often involves the revelation of the antagonist or the solution to a puzzle that has driven the plot forward. For instance, Agatha Christie's "Murder on the Orient Express" climaxes with Hercule Poirot's unmasking of the murderer, weaving together intricate clues and motives.

How a climax impacts readers can differ significantly based on its execution and presentation. An effectively crafted climax evokes strong emotional responses, whether joy, sadness, fear, or surprise. Readers form emotional connections with characters through these climactic moments, which can leave lasting impressions long after the book is finished. Consider the powerful climax of John Steinbeck's "Of Mice and Men," where George makes a heartbreaking decision regarding Lennie. This scene elicits profound empathy from readers and prompts reflection on themes of friendship, mercy, and sacrifice.

Ultimately, the climax is more than just the highest point of action; it's a lens through which we understand characters' true natures, moral dilemmas, and the overarching message of the narrative. By analysing how authors construct their climaxes, students can better appreciate storytelling techniques and how these key moments resonate on both intellectual and emotional levels.

Teachers can use these insights to foster classroom discussions, encouraging students to dissect climactic scenes and consider their broader implications. Such analysis enhances literary comprehension and critical thinking, equipping students with the skills to engage deeply with texts. For young adult readers, understanding the mechanics of the climax can transform their reading experience, allowing them to anticipate and appreciate narrative twists and the culmination of character journeys.

Falling Action and Resolution

Imagine you're nearing the end of a captivating novel. The gripping climax has just unfolded, leaving you on the edge of your seat. Now comes the falling action, a crucial part of narrative structure that gently guides the story towards resolution, tying up loose threads and providing closure.

Falling action immediately follows the climax, marking the beginning of the end of the story's central conflict. This phase allows characters to reflect on the ramifications of the climax, often leading to significant emotional processing and decisions that shape the outcome. For instance, in J.K. Rowling's "Harry Potter and the Goblet of Fire," the fallout from Voldemort's return is explored in the falling action as characters grapple with the new reality and prepare for what lies ahead.

The role of falling action is multifaceted. It not only serves to transition from the peak intensity of the climax but also helps ground the reader by resolving any remaining subplots or character arcs. It is a time when characters might confront their inner demons, reconcile with others, or make peace with the outcomes of the climax. In Harper Lee's "To Kill a Mockingbird," following the tension-filled court trial, the falling action sees Scout and Jem processing the events and understanding complex social issues better, essential for the story's resolution.

Following the falling action, we move into the resolution, the story's conclusion. The resolution is where all narrative threads are neatly tied up, providing closure for the characters and the readers. A well-crafted resolution offers satisfaction and a deeper insight into the themes and journeys explored throughout the narrative. For example, in George Orwell's "1984," the resolution provides a chilling conclusion that leaves readers pondering the implications of totalitarianism and control long after the last page is turned.

Resolutions come in many forms. Some stories opt for a tidy conclusion, summarising every plot point clearly and decisively. Jane Austen's novels often conclude with resolutions that leave few questions unanswered, ensuring readers see exactly how each character's journey concludes. An example can be found in "Pride and Prejudice," where Elizabeth Bennet and Mr. Darcy's romantic storyline reaches a satisfying end, fulfilling the expectations set throughout the narrative.

Conversely, some authors choose ambiguous or open-ended resolutions, encouraging readers to speculate and draw their conclusions. In Franz Kafka's "The Trial," the ending is deliberately obscure, reflecting the novel's themes of existential dread and the enigmatic nature of bureaucratic systems. Such endings can evoke robust emotional responses, ranging from frustration to intrigue, prompting readers to revisit and rethink the story long after finishing it.

Comparing different resolutions across genres can provide fascinating insights into how various literary traditions approach the end of a narrative. For instance, in the realm of mystery novels, like Agatha Christie's "Murder on the Orient Express," resolutions often reveal intricate details and cleverly hidden clues, offering a satisfying "aha" moment for readers. In contrast, literary fiction, such as Gabriel Garcia Marquez's "One Hundred Years of Solitude," may offer more poetic or cyclical conclusions, reflecting the genre's thematic depth and stylistic choices.

Fantasy and science fiction genres often feature resolutions that balance grand overarching plots and individual character arcs. In J.R.R. Tolkien's "The Lord of the Rings," the resolution not only addresses the fate of Middle-earth but also focuses on the personal journeys of characters like Frodo and Sam, blending epic and intimate storytelling elements. Such resolutions are designed to leave readers feeling fulfilled, having travelled alongside characters through their trials and triumphs.

Exploring the diversity in literary outcomes enriches our understanding of narrative techniques and their impact on reader experience. Whether neat or ambiguous, a well-executed resolution can resonate deeply with readers, reinforcing the story's themes and emotional undertones. This interplay between falling action and resolution underscores the deliberate craft of concluding a narrative, ensuring the journey feels complete and meaningful.

What We Learnt

In this chapter, we have explored the essential elements of plot structure in novels, focusing on how the exposition and inciting incident set the stage for a compelling narrative. By examining various examples from well-known works, we've seen how authors introduce characters, establish settings, and create situations that draw readers into the story. The inciting incident acts as a catalyst, disrupting the initial equilibrium and propelling the protagonist into the main action, engaging the reader's curiosity and interest right from the start.

Understanding these foundational components is crucial for anyone studying literature or aspiring to write stories. Recognising how the exposition and inciting incident function helps analyse and appreciate the craft behind novel writing. It also equips readers with the tools to engage more deeply with texts, enhancing their comprehension and enjoyment. For educators, these insights can serve as valuable teaching aids, fostering a richer classroom discussion about narrative techniques and their impact. Through this structured approach, we can all gain a greater appreciation for the intricate art of storytelling.

CHAPTER VII

Characterisation

"Creating memorable characters is vital for any storyteller, as compelling characters are the heart of any narrative. Bringing characters to life involves understanding and utilising several techniques that make them stand out and resonate with readers. Characters breathe life into the story, making it more engaging and relatable. Characterisation transforms a simple plot into a multi-dimensional world of dynamic interactions and emotional depth when done effectively."

This chapter will delve into various strategies for crafting unforgettable characters. We'll explore the differences between static and dynamic characters and how each can be used to enhance your narrative. Additionally, we'll discuss flat versus round characters, examining how their complexity contributes to the story's richness. By the end of this chapter, you'll have a deeper understanding of these character types and their roles in storytelling, providing you with the tools needed to create characters that indeed come alive on the page.

Static vs. Dynamic Characters

Understanding the distinction between static and dynamic characters is crucial for grasping their roles in literature. As the name suggests, static characters remain essentially unchanged throughout the narrative. They often serve as a constant presence, providing stability to the storyline. While they may lack development, their unchanging nature can highlight the transformations around them. For example, characters like Hagrid and Professor McGonagall remain the same in J.K. Rowling's "Harry Potter" series. Their consistency helps anchor the story's fantastical elements, serving as a touchstone for both the protagonist and the readers.

Static characters play significant roles by emphasising themes or moral points without undergoing personal change. Take Atticus Finch from Harper Lee's To Kill a Mockingbird. He remains steadfastly moral and just throughout the novel, emphasising the book's integrity and social justice themes. His unwavering principles spotlight other characters' growth and learning arcs, such as Scout and Jem.

On the other hand, dynamic characters undergo significant growth or change throughout the narrative. These characters face conflicts that prompt development, making their journeys relatable and engaging for the audience. Elizabeth Bennet from Jane Austen's "Pride and Prejudice" is a quintessential dynamic character. She evolves significantly from her initial prejudices toward Mr. Darcy, gaining self-awareness and understanding that lead to personal growth. Through her journey, readers experience the unfolding of deeper themes about pride, misconceptions, and personal development.

Dynamic characters often evoke emotional investment because they mirror human experiences of change and adaptation. In Charles Dickens's "A Christmas Carol," Ebenezer Scrooge's transformation from a miserly old man to a benevolent figure is central to the story. His journey through self-reflection, prompted by the visits of three ghosts, creates a powerful narrative about redemption and the capacity for change, stirring deep emotions in readers.

This understanding of static and dynamic characters enhances appreciation of their roles within a story. Static characters help establish enduring themes and provide a stable background against which the dynamic characters can evolve. In contrast, dynamic characters draw readers into an emotional engagement with their trials and transformations. The interaction between these two types of characters enriches the narrative, making it more compelling and multidimensional.

Analysing protagonists and antagonists from various novels can help practice identifying static and dynamic traits. Let's consider "The Great Gatsby" by F. Scott Fitzgerald. Nick Carraway, the novel's narrator, remains unchanged, maintaining his role as an observer and commentator. His static nature contrasts sharply with Gatsby's dynamic character, whose journey from a poor soldier to a wealthy but tragic figure drives the plot forward. This juxtaposition illustrates how static characters can frame and support the arcs of dynamic ones.

Another example is found in George Orwell's 1984. Winston Smith undergoes drastic changes in response to Big Brother's oppressive regime. His transformation from a disillusioned but hopeful individual to a broken and subjugated one underscores the theme of totalitarianism's devastating effects. On the flip side, characters like O'Brien and Julia exhibit much less change, serving to either reinforce the dystopian world or illuminate Winston's dynamic arc.

Examining literature through this lens deepens understanding and enables readers to appreciate the varied functions characters serve within a narrative. Recognising these distinctions makes discussions about literature more prosperous and more insightful. For educators, highlighting such differences can help students engage more deeply with texts, fostering critical thinking skills and a nuanced appreciation of storytelling techniques.

Authors strategically use static and dynamic characters to balance their narratives. Static characters might seem simplistic at first glance, but their enduring nature provides necessary context and stability within the story. Meanwhile, the evolving paths of dynamic characters offer readers a window into the complexities of human nature, reflecting real-life experiences and universal truths.

Analysing specific examples from literature makes it easier to understand how static and dynamic characters function within a story. Consider the relationship between Sherlock Holmes and Dr John Watson in Arthur Conan Doyle's detective series. Though extraordinary in his methods, Holmes remains relatively unchanged in brilliance and eccentricity, while Watson often grows and adapts through their adventures. This interplay highlights Holmes's genius and anchors the reader in Watson's more relatable perspective.

Flat vs. Round Characters

Understanding the distinctions between flat and round characters is crucial in mastering characterisation, as these differences significantly contribute to a story's depth and complexity.

Flat characters are typically simple, embodying a single dominant trait or characteristic defining their role in the story. These characters often serve as comedic relief or plot devices, helping to push the narrative forward without demanding much focus from the audience. For instance, think of a character who always appears cheerful and optimistic, no matter the situation. This simplicity allows readers to quickly understand their function in the story without expending cognitive resources to understand their motivations or emotional depth. Flat characters help maintain clarity and can provide a valuable foil to more complicated characters by highlighting their complexities.

In contrast, round characters are multi-dimensional, displaying a range of emotions and experiences that give them a sense of realism and relatability. A single trait does not just define these characters; they possess various characteristics that can sometimes be contradictory. A round character might sometimes be brave yet vulnerable or confident yet insecure. This diversity adds layers to their persona, making them appear more like real people. For example, a protagonist who starts as self-righteous but later reveals insecurities about their abilities, navigating through various internal conflicts, becomes someone the audience can root for or relate to. Round characters enrich the narrative by offering depth and an opportunity for readers to connect personally.

Each character type serves distinct functions within a narrative. Flat characters play supportive roles, providing context or enhancing themes without overshadowing the main storyline. They are akin to the supporting cast in a play, essential but not distracting. Their predictability can also comfort the audience by providing stable touchpoints in the story. In contrast, round characters drive the narrative forward through the challenges they encounter and their growth. Their struggles reflect broader themes within the story, such as the battle between good and evil, the journey toward self-discovery, or the complexity of human relationships. Through their development, round characters explore profound questions and universal truths, engaging the reader on a deeper level.

Creating round characters involves various techniques that add to their depth and relatability. One such technique is the development of a comprehensive backstory. A character's past can illuminate their current behaviour and motivations, making their actions more understandable and compelling. For instance, learning that a seemingly tough character had a difficult childhood can make their defensive demeanour more sympathetic. Backstories should be carefully crafted to align with the character's current traits and the story's themes, providing a rich tapestry that enhances the character's believability.

Another essential technique is the establishment of clear motivations. Characters must have reasons behind their actions, desires, and goals that resonate with readers. Motivations can stem from personal desires, moral beliefs, or external pressures, and they must be strong enough to drive the character's decisions throughout the plot. For example, a character motivated to protect their family will act differently than one driven by ambition or revenge. Clear motivations create coherence and purpose in a character's arc, making their journey through the story more engaging and logical.

Conflicts are another vital component in rounding out a character. Internal and external conflicts force characters to confront their limitations, question their beliefs, and grow. Internal conflicts involve struggles within a character, such as dealing with guilt, fear, or indecision. External conflicts involve challenges outside the character, including antagonists, societal pressures, or physical obstacles. The interplay between these conflicts and the character's responses provides significant narrative tension and propels character development. For example, a character facing a villain's external threat and inner doubts about their ability to overcome that threat becomes far more intriguing and relatable.

These techniques—backstory, motivations, and conflicts—contribute to creating round characters and enhance their depth and relatability. When readers understand where a character is coming from, why they do what they do, and how they handle challenges, they are likelier to form an emotional connection with them. This connection is crucial for maintaining reader engagement and investment in the story, as emotionally resonant characters make for a more compelling narrative.

Character Arcs and Development

Character arcs are essential tools in illustrating a character's growth and development. They provide readers with an immersive experience as they follow the protagonist's journey from beginning to end. At their core, character arcs reflect the challenges and transformations the characters face, making them memorable and relatable. Understanding these arcs allows readers to appreciate the depth of character development and recognise the underlying themes within a narrative.

A character arc maps out the path a character travels throughout the story, highlighting significant moments contributing to their growth. This journey often begins with the character in relative normalcy, only to be disrupted by events that challenge their worldview and abilities. As the story progresses, the character undergoes various trials that test their resolve, ultimately leading to a transformation or realisation. This progression makes the character more engaging and reinforces the story's themes and messages.

One way to analyse character arcs is through common arc types like the Hero's Journey and the Tragic Arc. The

Hero's Journey, popularised by Joseph Campbell, provides a framework for understanding a character's growth through a series of stages, including the call to adventure, crossing the threshold, facing trials, and achieving transformation. For example, in J.K. Rowling's Harry Potter series, Harry's journey follows this arc. He transitions from a young boy unaware of his magical heritage to a hero confronting and defeating dark forces. The Hero's Journey emphasises redemption and self-discovery, making it a powerful tool for analysing character development.

In contrast, the Tragic Arc focuses on a character's decline, often due to a fatal flaw or external pressures. This arc typically leads to a downfall, starkly contrasting the redemptive nature of the Hero's Journey. William Shakespeare's Macbeth exemplifies a Tragic Arc, as Macbeth's ambition and desire for power drive him to betrayal and murder, ultimately leading to his demise. By examining different arc types, readers can distinguish between stories of redemption and those depicting downfall, gaining a deeper understanding of the narrative's direction and purpose.

Conflict is crucial in driving character change, acting as a catalyst for evolution and decision-making. Both internal and external conflicts are essential in shaping a character's development. Internal conflicts involve the character grappling with personal dilemmas, fears, or desires, often leading to significant growth and self-awareness. For instance, Elizabeth Bennet in Jane Austen's Pride and Prejudice faces internal conflict as she navigates her prejudices and misunderstandings about Mr. Darcy, resulting in her eventual realisation and growth.

External conflicts, on the other hand, arise from challenges posed by outside forces, such as antagonists, societal expectations, or environmental obstacles. These conflicts force characters to adapt, make difficult choices, and demonstrate resilience. In Suzanne Collins's The Hunger Games, Katniss Everdeen confronts numerous external conflicts, including survival in the arena and defiance against an oppressive regime. These struggles highlight her strength and resourcefulness, contributing to her character development.

One must note changes in behaviour, motivations, and relationships throughout the story to track character development effectively. Observing how a character evolves in response to conflict and experiences can enhance analytical skills and engagement with the narrative. For example, in Harper Lee's To Kill a Mockingbird, Scout Finch's growth is evident through her changing perceptions of race, justice, and morality. Initially naive and impressionable, Scout learns valuable lessons from her father, Atticus, and the events surrounding Tom Robinson's trial, leading to a more nuanced understanding of her world.

Tracking these changes requires careful attention to specific moments in the story where the character exhibits growth or regression. This might include fundamental interactions, pivotal events, or shifts in the character's outlook. By documenting these instances, readers can create a comprehensive picture of the character's arc, identifying patterns and turning points that define their journey. Additionally, noting any shifts in the character's relationships with others can provide further insight into their development. Relationships often mirror the character's inner changes and reveal their evolving attitudes and values.

For instance, in Charles Dickens's A Christmas Carol, Ebenezer Scrooge's transformation is marked by his changed behaviour towards those around him. Initially a miserly and cold-hearted man, Scrooge's encounters with the ghosts of Christmas Past, Present, and Future prompt a profound shift in his demeanour. His newfound generosity and warmth towards his employees and family signify the completion of his character arc, demonstrating the impact of introspection and redemption.

By employing these techniques, readers can engage more deeply with the narrative and appreciate the intricacies of character development. Tracking changes in behaviour, motivations, and relationships enhances analytical skills and fosters a greater connection to the characters.

Dialogue and Voice

Dialogue and character voice are essential for creating vibrant, memorable characters that leap off the page. Authentic dialogue serves as a window into a character's soul, reflecting their background, motivations, and emotional state. When done well, it can immerse readers in the story and reveal underlying themes without overt explanation.

Consider a character from a working-class background. Their speech might include regional dialects, idioms, and colloquialisms, which can give clues about their upbringing and worldview. For example, a character who grew up in the southern United States might use phrases like "y'all" and "bless your heart," which convey geographical and cultural context. This authentic manner of speaking helps build a more prosperous, multi-faceted identity for the character, allowing readers to connect more deeply with them.

Character voice is another critical component of characterisation that adds depth and differentiation. Each character's unique way of expressing themselves should be consistent throughout the narrative. Think of the sarcastic detective who always has a witty comeback or the shy teenager whose sentences often trail off awkwardly. These distinct voices make characters stand out and become more relatable to the reader.

When constructing dialogue, it's essential to consider how each line serves the dual purpose of revealing character traits and advancing the plot. Dialogue should never feel aimless; it pushes the narrative forward by creating tension, unveiling secrets, or resolving conflicts. Imagine a scene where two estranged siblings are forced to confront past grievances during a family gathering. Their conversation could escalate existing tensions ("You never cared about me!"), reveal hidden motives ("I took the job because I had no choice!"), or resolve long-standing issues ("I'm sorry for what happened..."). These exchanges do more than fill pages—they provide crucial turning points that drive the story forward.

One must pay close attention to patterns, subtext, and interruptions to dissect dialogue effectively. Patterns in speech can indicate habitual thought processes or emotional states. For instance, a character frequently repeating specific phrases or questions might imply insecurity or doubt. Subtext—the meaning behind the words—adds another layer of complexity. A seemingly mundane exchange about the weather can be tense if the characters use it to avoid discussing a more pressing issue.

Interruptions in dialogue can serve multiple functions: heighten the drama, suggest reluctant communication, or reveal power dynamics between characters. For example, a boss interrupting an employee mid-sentence showcases authority and dominance, while mutual interruptions in a heated argument can elevate emotional stakes. Analysing these interruptions helps readers appreciate the subtleties of the author's craft, making the dialogue more engaging and meaningful.

Understanding these techniques enriches the reading experience by allowing students to identify and appreciate the nuances of character dialogue and voice. These insights provide valuable teaching points for educators when guiding students through literary analysis. By examining authentic dialogue, character voice, and the role of dialogue in advancing the plot, students and teachers can develop a deeper appreciation for the intricacies of characterisation in literature.

What We Learnt

Understanding the different types of characters in literature, whether static, dynamic, flat, or round, allows readers to appreciate the layers and depth within a narrative. Static characters provide stability and highlight the growth around them, while dynamic characters take us on a journey of change and self-discovery. Similarly, flat characters serve as straightforward roles that support the story's progression, whereas round characters offer a rich tapestry of traits that make them feel real and relatable.

By examining these character types and their functions through examples from beloved novels, we can see how authors skillfully craft characters to drive the plot and reinforce themes. This knowledge enhances our engagement with stories, encouraging us to delve deeper into the motivations, conflicts, and developments of each character we encounter. Whether you are a student, teacher, or avid reader, recognising these distinctions will enrich your literary experience and deepen your enjoyment of storytelling.

CHAPTER VIII

Setting and Atmosphere

"Setting and atmosphere in storytelling are crucial elements that shape the reader's experience. When an author crafts a vivid setting, they are not just providing a backdrop for the characters but also creating an environment that can profoundly enhance the narrative. A story's physical and temporal aspects set the stage for everything that unfolds, influencing the plot's mood, tone, and direction. From an ancient city's bustling streets to a small village's quiet corners, each setting offers unique character development and thematic exploration opportunities."

This chapter will explore how different settings impact the narrative and bring stories to life. We will explore how authors use descriptive imagery to create mental landscapes that resonate with readers on an emotional level. By examining famous literary works, you'll see examples of how sensory details evoke specific moods and atmospheres. Additionally, we will discuss the significance of temporal settings, such as historical eras and periods, and how they influence the motivations and behaviours of characters. Prepare to understand better how the artful depiction of settings can enrich your reading experience and enhance your analytical skills.

Descriptive Imagery

Descriptive imagery is a powerful storytelling tool, possessing the unique ability to transport readers into the very heart of a narrative. By leveraging vivid descriptions, authors can create mental representations that resonate emotionally with readers, often evoking strong feelings. This engagement fosters a deeper connection to the story and its characters, ultimately enriching the reading experience.

Compelling imagery engages all five senses, making narratives come alive in the reader's mind. For instance, consider the way Charles Dickens paints a scene in *Great Expectations*. When Pip first encounters Miss Havisham in her decaying mansion, Dickens doesn't just describe the room; he immerses the reader with visual cues and olfactory hints. These sensory details not only sketch a vivid picture but also evoke an eerie mood that permeates the entire scene, letting readers almost smell the decay and feel the coldness of the space. This sensory immersion ties readers closely to Pip's emotions and the unsettling atmosphere, making the scene memorable and enhancing their understanding of the narrative.

Imagery isn't limited to merely painting a picture—it supplements and elevates character development and plot situations. Take Harper Lee's *To Kill a Mockingbird* as an example. Lee uses descriptive imagery to capture the sleepy town of Maycomb, Alabama. She writes, "Maycomb was an old town, but it was a tired old town when I first knew it." Through this simple yet evocative description, readers can almost see the worn-out streets and sense the slow-moving pace of life. This setting is a backdrop for the unfolding events, framing the racial tensions and social dynamics central to the novel. All these elements work together to create a rich tapestry that enhances the narrative and the thematic depth.

Analysing excerpts from famous novels can further illustrate how descriptive imagery is a storytelling tool. In J.K. Rowling's *Harry Potter* series, the author masterfully uses detailed descriptions to construct the magical world of Hogwarts. With its enchanted ceiling, floating candles, and long house tables, the Great Hall comes vividly to life through her words. This immersive environment not only captivates the reader's imagination but also provides a tangible setting where the characters' adventures unfold, enhancing the overall magic and wonder of the story.

Recognising the importance of sensory details in storytelling is crucial for any aspiring writer or literature student. Sensory language does more than set a scene; it creates an atmosphere that can provoke strong emotional responses. An evocative description of a stormy night can generate tension and foreboding, while a sunny meadow might invoke a sense of peace and tranquillity. This atmospheric groundwork lays the foundation for emotional engagement, drawing readers deeper into the narrative and making them feel like they are part of the story.

Powerful sensory language plays a significant role in forging an emotional connection between the reader and the narrative. For example, in the novel *The Book Thief* by Markus Zusak, the author often uses colour to convey mood and emotion. When describing the sky during a bombing raid, Zusak writes, "The sky was the colour of Jews." This stark and poignant imagery evokes a visceral reaction, embedding the scene into the reader's memory and highlighting the gravity of the situation. Such use of sensory language not only enhances the overall atmosphere but also deepens the emotional impact on the reader.

Guidelines for using sensory details effectively can assist writers aiming to craft compelling narratives. They should strive to incorporate multiple senses into their descriptions without overwhelming the reader. Instead of focusing solely on what characters see, writers can include sounds, smells, textures, and tastes to build a more immersive experience. For instance, instead of merely stating that a character walks into a forest, a writer could describe the crunch of leaves underfoot, the scent of pine in the air, the sound of birdsong, and the cool dampness of the ground. These layered details can transform a simple setting into a vivid, multi-sensory experience that draws readers in.

Furthermore, descriptive imagery can set the tone before any actions unfold, guiding reader expectations. In F. Scott Fitzgerald's *The Great Gatsby*, the luxury of Gatsby's parties is described in such detail that readers can almost hear the jazz music, taste the champagne, and feel the crowd's energy. This lavish setting establishes the tone of excess and superficiality throughout the novel, preparing readers for the underlying themes of wealth, ambition, and disillusionment.

Temporal and Geographical Settings

When discussing setting in literature, we describe the time and place where the story unfolds. These elements are crucial in shaping the narrative, how characters behave, and what themes emerge.

First, consider how different eras influence the characters and plot. Each period comes with its unique cultural context—think of Victorian England's strict social class systems or the revolutionary fervour of 18th-century France. These historical backdrops inform what drives the characters, their aspirations, and fears. For instance, a

Medieval European character might struggle with issues of feudal loyalty that wouldn't make sense in modern-day America. Cultural norms, technological advancements, and societal expectations vary greatly from one era to another, and these distinctions can significantly shape character motivations and plot developments.

The landscape and environment where stories unfold add more depth to the narrative. Imagine a tale set in the arid deserts of Arizona versus one in the lush rainforests of the Amazon. The physical surroundings affect the mood and the character's actions. A character trekking through a desert may deal with heat, dehydration, and vast, empty spaces, symbolising isolation or an internal journey. In contrast, a rainforest setting might introduce challenges such as constant humidity, dense foliage, and a plethora of wildlife, creating a sense of entanglement and complexity in the character's life. The setting can reflect the characters' internal states, mirroring their emotional landscapes.

Temporal settings further impose restrictions or opportunities for the characters, shaping their journeys. Think about the limited communication methods before the invention of the telephone or the vast opportunities for travel after the advent of aeroplanes. Characters' choices and possibilities are deeply influenced by their time's technology and societal norms. For example, in a story set during World War II, characters might face rationing and blackouts, affecting their day-to-day lives and adding tension to the narrative. Temporal settings also help to anchor the plot's pacing, providing natural deadlines or milestones tied to historical events or time-specific activities like seasonal harvests or annual festivals.

Local culture and geography also significantly shape character interactions and community dynamics. Whether it's a small coastal town where everyone knows each other or a sprawling metropolis with strangers, the setting impacts how characters relate. In a close-knit community, characters might experience a sense of belonging or pressure to conform. At the same time, in a big city, they might face anonymity, loneliness, freedom, and opportunities. Geographic factors like proximity to water, mountains, or open plains can dictate livelihoods, leisure activities, and even conflict points within the story. For example, a fishing village's economy and daily routines revolve around the tides and seasons, affecting every character's life and decisions.

Enabling readers to identify successful descriptive techniques when reading independently is a crucial skill gleaned from understanding how settings operate. Tips include paying attention to how authors use location to reveal character traits or foreshadow events. One might notice consistent patterns like how urban settings often highlight themes of isolation despite crowded spaces or how rural settings can emphasise tradition and close-knit relationships.

Atmosphere and Mood

Though often used interchangeably, atmosphere and mood serve distinct functions in shaping a narrative's impact. Understanding these two elements' differences is crucial for fully appreciating how writers engage their readers. Atmosphere refers to the overarching feeling or environment within the text, crafted through detailed descriptions of setting, tone, and sensory details. Mood, conversely, pertains to the emotions felt by characters and, subsequently, the reader's emotional response to those experiences.

Imagine stepping into a haunted house. The creaky floors, dim lighting, and distant echoes create an eerie atmosphere that sets the stage for future events. This feeling primes the reader for suspenseful or frightening moments, laying the groundwork for expected reactions. Now, consider a character walking through this same haunted house. Their unease, fear, or determination to face whatever lies ahead shapes the mood. These emotions drive the character's actions and resonate with the reader, drawing them deeper into the story.

Atmospheric descriptions serve as essential tools for setting reader expectations. They foreshadow events and elicit specific emotional responses, guiding how the narrative unfolds. For instance, a story set in a bustling city filled with vibrant colours and lively street noises creates an atmosphere of energy and excitement. Readers anticipate dynamic encounters and fast-paced plot developments. Conversely, a tale unfolding in a quiet, foggy village might evoke a sense of mystery and anticipation for secrets yet to be revealed.

Authors use various techniques to craft distinctive atmospheres in their narratives, with tone and imagery being the most effective. Tone, the writer's attitude toward the subject, influences the atmosphere significantly. A cheerful tone can make a mundane setting feel warm and inviting, while a sombre tone can transform it into a gloomy backdrop. Imagery, the descriptive language that engages the senses, allows readers to see, hear, touch, taste, and smell the world within the story. When describing a scene, vivid imagery lets readers visualise the physical attributes and the mood enveloping the space.

Let's delve into some examples to illustrate these points. Consider a passage where the author describes a dense forest at dusk: "The sun dipped below the horizon, casting long shadows that danced among the trees. The rustle of leaves and distant calls of nocturnal creatures created a symphony of nature winding down." Here, the tone is serene and reflective, crafting an atmosphere of calm and transition. The imagery evokes the senses, allowing readers to feel the cool air and hear the sounds, immersing them in the setting.

Contrast this with another description: "Thunder rumbled in the distance as dark clouds gathered overhead. The wind howled through the skeletal trees, sending shivers down the spine." The tone here is ominous, and the imagery is foreboding, contributing to an atmosphere of tension and impending danger. These atmospheric cues prepare readers for events that will likely be intense and dramatic, priming their emotions accordingly.

Recognising shifts in atmosphere and mood is also critical, as these changes can reveal character development and highlight overarching themes. When an atmosphere transitions from light-hearted to oppressive, it may signal a turning point in the narrative, reflecting the protagonist's internal journey. For example, a character who starts their adventure in a sunny, open landscape might find themselves navigating dark alleyways as they face more significant obstacles. The shift in setting mirrors their growing challenges, emphasising the theme of perseverance against adversity.

Similarly, mood changes reflect the evolving emotions of characters. A character initially portrayed as confident might experience fear and doubt in certain situations. These emotional fluctuations add depth to the character and enhance the reader's engagement by providing a rollercoaster of feelings to experience alongside them. For instance, in J.K. Rowling's "Harry Potter" series, the mood often shifts from wonder and excitement at Hogwarts to fear and tension during confrontations with Voldemort and his followers. These shifts mirror Harry's growth from a curious student to a determined hero, underscoring themes of bravery and sacrifice.

To further understand these concepts, consider another literary example from Harper Lee's "To Kill a Mockingbird." The atmosphere of Maycomb, a small Southern town, is depicted through its slow pace, sweltering heat, and close-knit community dynamics. This atmosphere provides a backdrop for exploring themes of racism, morality, and justice. The mood shifts dramatically throughout the novel, particularly during the trial of Tom Robinson. Readers experience frustration, anger, and sadness, reflecting the deep moral conflicts the characters face.

Symbolism in Settings

In literature, settings serve a purpose beyond merely providing a backdrop for the storyline. They can operate symbolically, adding layers of meaning that enrich the narrative. Recognising these symbolic elements is crucial to understanding the depth and complexity of a novel.

Let's start with objects, colours, or locations within novels that take on symbolic significance. A red rose might symbolise love and passion, while a stormy sea could represent chaos and turmoil. When authors weave these symbols into their settings, they enhance the thematic resonance of the story. For instance, Charles Dickens's "Great Expectations" uses decaying mansions and murky marshes to reflect the themes of decay and moral corruption. By paying attention to these details, readers can gain insight into the underlying messages of the narrative.

Weather often plays a significant role in mirroring character emotions, creating an interconnection between the external and internal landscapes. A bright, sunny day might reflect a character's joy and optimism, whereas a dark, rainy night could mirror feelings of sadness and despair. This technique, called pathetic fallacy, can be seen in many classic works. In Emily Brontë's "Wuthering Heights," the turbulent weather on the moors parallels the volatile emotions and conflicts among the characters. Understanding this connection allows readers to experience the characters' emotions more vividly and better comprehend the story's emotional dynamics.

Seasonal changes within narratives can also signal transformations in the storyline or characters' progressions. Spring often symbolises rebirth and new beginnings, summer represents maturity and fulfilment, autumn signifies decline or change, and winter embodies death or stagnation. In F. Scott Fitzgerald's "The Great Gatsby," the transition from spring to summer highlights the peak and subsequent decline of Gatsby's dream and his relationship with Daisy. Seasons are not just time markers but also thematic tools that reinforce the narrative's progression and the characters' journeys.

Moreover, understanding symbolism in the setting enhances comprehension of deeper themes and nuances within the narrative. For example, in George Orwell's 1984, the oppressive and drab setting of Airstrip One reflects the bleakness and control exerted by the totalitarian regime. The grey, monotonous landscape supports the theme of dehumanisation and loss of individuality. As readers note these symbolic elements, they can appreciate the thematic depth and deliberate choices made by the author.

Take Mark Twain's "The Adventures of Huckleberry Finn." The Mississippi River is more than a physical setting; it symbolises freedom and adventure for Huck and Jim. It contrasts with the restrictive and hypocritical society on land. The changing scenery underscores their evolving perspectives and growing bond as they journey down the river. Recognising the river's symbolic significance helps readers understand the broader themes of freedom and societal critique woven throughout the narrative.

Symbolism can also manifest through cultural or historical landmarks within a story. In Harper Lee's "To Kill a Mockingbird," the Radley House represents fear and mystery to the children. Over time, as Scout and Jem come to understand Boo Radley, the house's symbolism shifts, reflecting the theme of overcoming prejudice and understanding others. These symbolic settings invite readers to look beyond the surface and explore the deeper meanings embedded in the narrative.

Literary symbolism extends to colour usage as well. Colours can evoke specific emotions and signify particular themes. In Nathaniel Hawthorne's "The Scarlet Letter," the letter 'A' embroidered in scarlet becomes a complex symbol of sin, guilt, and redemption. Red evokes shame and passion, encapsulating Hester Prynne's experiences and societal judgment. By interpreting these colour symbols, readers can uncover layers of meaning that contribute to their understanding of the characters and themes.

Understanding how settings operate symbolically enables readers to engage with the text more deeply. It allows them to see beyond the literal and appreciate authors' deliberate choices to convey complex ideas and emotions. Through carefully observing symbolic settings, readers can unlock new dimensions of interpretation and enrich their literary experience.

Consider how J.K. Rowling uses setting in the Harry Potter series. Places like Hogwarts and the Forbidden Forest are imbued with symbolic meaning. Hogwarts represents safety, learning, and growth, while the Forbidden Forest symbolises danger, mystery, and the unknown. These settings help shape the narrative and deepen readers' engagement with the story's themes and characters.

Readers can better understand the narrative by recognising the symbolic significance of settings, whether through objects, weather patterns, seasonal changes, or colours. They become more attuned to how authors use settings to convey themes, emotions, and character development. This deeper comprehension ultimately enhances their appreciation of literature and ability to analyse and discuss texts critically.

What We Learnt

In this chapter, we've delved into the significance of setting in storytelling. By examining how descriptive imagery, temporal settings, and geographical locations shape narratives, we see how these elements create vibrant backdrops that enhance character development and thematic depth. From Charles Dickens' decaying mansion in *Great Expectations* to the bustling city streets in F. Scott Fitzgerald's *The Great Gatsby*, detailed settings bring stories to life and evoke strong emotional responses from readers.

Understanding the interplay between atmosphere, mood, and symbolism in settings allows us to appreciate literature more deeply. Whether through the sensory details that make a scene vivid or the symbolic meanings embedded in landscapes and objects, settings serve as powerful tools for storytelling. By recognising these techniques, we can better analyse and discuss literary works, enriching our reading experience and fostering a greater connection with the narratives we explore.

CHAPTER IX

Themes and Motifs

"Identifying and analysing themes and motifs within novels is critical to unlocking the deeper meanings embedded in literary texts. Just as a theme represents an author's broader message, motifs are recurring symbols or concepts that reinforce these thematic elements throughout the narrative. Readers who grasp these components gain access to the universal truths and social commentaries that lie beneath the story's surface, enriching their understanding and appreciation of literature."

This chapter will define themes and motifs, distinguishing between these two necessary literary devices. We'll explore examples from well-known novels to illustrate how themes and motifs work together to enhance the reader's experience. Moreover, we'll discuss strategies for identifying and connecting these elements within a text, providing practical tools to uncover patterns and deeper meanings in your reading. Whether you're a student aiming to improve your literary analysis skills, an educator seeking to guide your students, or a young adult reader curious about diving deeper into novels, this chapter offers valuable insights and techniques to elevate your understanding of literary works.

Defining Themes and Motifs

Understanding the concepts of "theme" and "motif" is crucial for anyone studying literature, as these elements are fundamental to grasping the more profound meaning within a story. A theme in literature represents the underlying message or central idea that the author intends to convey. It goes beyond the narrative's surface to offer insight into universal truths or social commentaries that resonate with readers. For instance, the theme of "love conquers all" can be found in countless novels, from Shakespeare's "Romeo and Juliet" to Jane Austen's "Pride and Prejudice," each exploring different facets of love yet conveying a similar overarching message.

Conversely, motifs are recurring elements, symbols, or concepts that reinforce a theme throughout a narrative. These can be images, sounds, actions, or other figures that have symbolic significance and contribute to the work's overall message. Unlike themes, which are broad and abstract, motifs tend to be more concrete and tangible. An example of a motif is the use of light and darkness in William Golding's "Lord of the Flies," which underscores the theme of civilisation versus savagery. The repeated references to light and dark create a vivid image and help emphasise the conflict between the characters' civilised instincts and their descent into barbarism.

Recognising motifs within a text can significantly aid readers in tracking and connecting themes across the storyline. Readers can uncover patterns that might otherwise go unnoticed by highlighting recurring elements. For example, F. Scott Fitzgerald's "The Great Gatsby" employs the motif of the green light at the end of Daisy's dock, symbolising Gatsby's unrelenting pursuit of the American Dream. This recurring image helps readers see how Gatsby's dreams drive the narrative forward and connect to the broader theme of aspiration and the pitfalls of pursuing an unattainable ideal.

Another critical aspect of understanding motifs is seeing how they interweave with themes to enrich the reader's experience. When motifs are used effectively, they do more than repeat—they highlight and emphasise critical aspects of the text, making the thematic content more accessible and memorable. Consider J.K. Rowling's "Harry Potter" series, in which the motif of "the scar" serves multiple purposes. It marks Harry as unique and symbolises his connection to the antagonist, Voldemort, reinforcing the themes of destiny and the struggle against evil. Each time the scar is mentioned, it brings readers back to these broader ideas, making the narrative more cohesive and impactful.

One way to track motifs is to note when certain elements recur and consider why the author chose to include them at those specific points in the story. For example, in George Orwell's 1984, the motif of "Big Brother" is omnipresent, symbolising the constant surveillance and control exerted by the totalitarian regime. Every mention of Big Brother reminds the reader of the oppressive power structure and reinforces the theme of loss of individuality and freedom under such a government.

Furthermore, understanding this interplay between motifs and themes can deepen our appreciation of literature by revealing the layers of meaning authors embed in their works. For instance, in Gabriel Garcia Marquez's "One Hundred Years of Solitude," the motif of cyclical time—evident in the repetitive names and events within the Buendía family—underscores the theme of inevitable fate. This motif highlights the inescapable nature of history and personal destiny and connects individual experiences to a larger cosmic order.

Common Universal Themes

Love, in its many forms, is perhaps the most universal theme in literature. From timeless romances like "Pride and Prejudice" to the intense familial love in "To Kill a Mockingbird," writers use love to explore the depth of human emotions. Romantic love often forms the foundation for many novels depicting the trials and triumphs of relationships. Consider Shakespeare's "Romeo and Juliet," where romantic love is paramount, yet so are themes of familial conflict and societal expectations.

On the other hand, familial love offers a different perspective grounded in kinship and growth. In novels like "Little Women" by Louisa May Alcott, readers witness the bond between siblings, showcasing the strength and resilience that familial love brings. Similarly, platonic love, which focuses on deep friendships, allows authors to explore loyalty, trust, and companionship. "The Lord of the Rings" series exemplifies this through the enduring friendship between Frodo and Sam, emphasising that love doesn't always need a romantic angle to be profound and impactful.

Conflict is another driving force in literature, shaping narratives and offering insight into characters' lives and decisions. Conflict can be internal, involving a character's struggle with their desires or beliefs, or external, pitting characters against each other or larger social forces. For instance, Herman Melville's "Moby Dick" showcases Captain Ahab's relentless internal conflict, blending his obsession with revenge against the white whale with his deteriorating mental state. Conversely, external conflict is prominently featured in George Orwell's "1984," where protagonist Winston Smith grapples with a repressive regime, highlighting themes of control, rebellion, and the human spirit's resilience.

Through conflict, characters evolve, revealing layers of their personalities and triggering transformations. This evolution often leads to critical self-realisation and growth, making it a key element in narrative progression. Such conflicts engage readers, allowing them to empathise with characters and delve into the complexities of human nature.

Another vital literary theme is identity, offering a window into the inner workings of characters' minds and their quests for self-discovery. Characters embarking on journeys of personal growth confront societal norms, personal doubts, and inner conflicts, inevitably leading to evolution. This quest for identity is vividly illustrated in J.D. Salinger's "The Catcher in the Rye." Holden Caulfield's struggles highlight the confusion and angst associated with adolescence, representing a universal search for meaning and authenticity.

Identity themes extend beyond individual journeys, often reflecting broader social issues like race, gender, and class. Addressing such topics enables literature to foster empathy and understanding among readers. For example, Toni Morrison's "The Bluest Eye" delves into themes of racial identity and beauty standards, portraying the devastating impact of societal pressures on African American girls. This exploration encourages readers to reflect on their perceptions and biases, promoting a deeper understanding of diverse experiences.

Similarly, James Baldwin's works, such as "Giovanni's Room," examine sexual identity issues and societal acceptance. Baldwin's nuanced portrayal of his characters' struggles with their identities urges readers to consider the complexities and challenges faced by those whose identities do not conform to societal norms. These themes resonate deeply, prompting readers to contemplate their own identities and the identities of those around them.

Themes of identity also address gender issues, providing a platform to challenge traditional roles and stereotypes. Margaret Atwood's "The Handmaid's Tale" explores gender and power dynamics, critiquing patriarchal structures and advocating for women's autonomy. Through the protagonist Offred, Atwood exposes the oppressive mechanisms that strip away women's identities, calling for resistance and change. Such narratives are instrumental in generating discourse on gender equality and inspiring readers to question and challenge societal norms.

Moreover, themes of identity often intersect with class, shedding light on economic disparities and social hierarchies. Charles Dickens's "Great Expectations" is a prime example, exploring the protagonist Pip's aspirations and the influence of wealth and status on his identity. The novel critiques the rigid class structures of Victorian England, encouraging readers to ponder the implications of social mobility and the true nature of success.

Recurring Motifs Across Genres

Throughout literature, motifs are recurring elements that enhance readers' understanding of themes and character development. Recognising these motifs across different genres can provide a deeper appreciation for the narrative's complexity and significance.

Nature is one of the most prevalent motifs found in various literary genres. It often acts as a mirror reflecting characters' emotions and the thematic elements at play. For instance, a storm might symbolise turmoil or emotional chaos in a character's life, while a serene landscape could represent inner peace or contentment. In Emily Brontë's "Wuthering Heights," the wild and untamed moorlands reflect Heathcliff and Catherine's passionate and tumultuous relationship. The moors symbolise their love's raw and untamed nature, emphasising the intense emotional experiences the characters share. By examining how authors use nature to parallel their characters' internal states, readers can gain insight into unspoken feelings and underlying conflicts within the narrative.

Another common motif is the journey, which symbolises physical or emotional transformation. This motif can manifest as a literal voyage, such as Odysseus's long journey home in Homer's "The Odyssey," or as a symbolic journey toward self-discovery and growth, as seen in "To Kill a Mockingbird" by Harper Lee. Scout Finch's journey throughout the novel represents her path from innocence to a mature understanding of human nature's and social justice's complexities. The journey motif highlights the protagonist's trials and tribulations, marking significant change and personal development points. It provides a framework for readers to track the character's evolution and understand the transformative experiences that shape their identity and worldview.

Light and darkness serve as potent symbols representing good and evil, knowledge and ignorance. Authors frequently use this motif to create stark contrasts and highlight moral dilemmas within their narratives. In Joseph Conrad's "Heart of Darkness," darkness symbolises the unknown horrors of colonial exploitation and the moral ambiguity the characters face. Conversely, light often signifies hope, enlightenment, and purity. For example, in F. Scott Fitzgerald's "The Great Gatsby," the green light at the end of Daisy Buchanan's dock represents Gatsby's hopes and dreams for a future with Daisy, despite the moral corruption surrounding them. By analysing instances where light and darkness appear within a story, readers can better understand the author's ethical undertones and thematic messages.

Examining these motifs fosters a deeper understanding of character motivations and moral implications. Characters are often driven by forces emblematic of the motifs present in their stories. For instance, in J.R.R. Tolkien's "The Lord of the Rings," the ring motif represents power and its corrupting influence. The characters' varying reactions to the ring reveal their inner struggles and moral fortitude. Despite the immense burden it places on him, Frodo's determination to destroy the ring underscores his selflessness and resilience. Meanwhile, Gollum's obsession with the ring highlights his descent into madness and moral degradation. Understanding these dynamics allows readers to grasp the complexities of the character's motivations and the ethical questions they grapple with.

In addition to individual character analysis, recognising motifs can offer insights into the broader societal and cultural contexts depicted in novels. In Toni Morrison's "Beloved," the motif of haunting ghosts reflects the lingering trauma of slavery and its impact on African American communities. The ghost of Sethe's deceased daughter, Beloved, embodies the unresolved pain and suffering experienced by those who endured slavery. By engaging with such motifs, readers can uncover layers of meaning related to historical and social issues, enriching their overall interpretation of the text.

Moreover, identifying motifs can enhance readers' appreciation of an author's craft and stylistic choices. When authors strategically employ motifs, they create a cohesive and resonant narrative that reinforces crucial themes and messages. For example, in Gabriel García Márquez's "One Hundred Years of Solitude," the recurring motif of cyclical time reflects the repetitive nature of the Buendía family's history and their inability to escape past mistakes. This motif underscores the theme of fate versus free will and highlights the novel's intricate structure. Readers can appreciate the deliberate and skilful ways authors weave complex narratives and convey profound ideas by paying attention to these motifs.

Understanding common motifs can also help readers connect themes across different works of literature. For instance, the journey motif appears in various forms in numerous literary texts, from epic poems to modern novels. By recognising this motif in works such as "The Catcher in the Rye" and "The Hobbit," readers can draw parallels between Holden Caulfield's quest for identity and Bilbo Baggins's adventure towards self-realisation. Such connections foster a more comprehensive and nuanced understanding of literary traditions and the universality of specific experiences and themes.

Interplay Between Theme and Plot

Themes are intricately woven into plot structures, affirming their relevance and function in storytelling. This relationship between themes and plots is fundamental to how stories unfold and resonate with readers. Themes can motivate character actions and drive the plot forward, establishing a deep connection between narrative elements and underlying messages.

Consider how a theme such as "redemption" shapes a novel. Characters within the story may be driven by past wrongdoings and seek opportunities to atone for their mistakes. These motivations propel the plot and allow readers to explore how individuals seek forgiveness and make amends. For example, in Victor Hugo's *Les Misérables*, Jean Valjean's journey from a hardened criminal to a compassionate caregiver is framed by his quest for redemption. This thematic underpinning drives many of the novel's pivotal moments, influencing his decisions and actions throughout the story.

Similarly, earlier events in the plot can foreshadow themes that will emerge later. Foreshadowing is a literary device often used to hint at future developments, providing subtle clues that enrich the reader's understanding of the story. In Harper Lee's *To Kill a Mockingbird*, early racial injustice and prejudice set the stage for the more prominent themes of moral growth and social inequality that unfold as the narrative progresses. By introducing these elements early on, the author prepares the reader to grasp the thematic depth that will define the characters' experiences and the novel's overall message.

The resolution of a story often culminates in the thematic message intended by the author. The climax and denouement combine various narrative threads, making the central themes crystallise and leaving a lasting impression on the reader. For instance, in George Orwell's *1984*, the resolution underscores the theme of totalitarianism and the loss of personal freedom. The protagonist's ultimate defeat is a bleak commentary on the oppressive power structures that govern society, driving home the thematic concerns permeating the novel.

Understanding these connections between themes and plot structures can help readers articulate their text interpretations. When readers recognise how themes motivate character actions, foreshadow key plot points, and culminate in the resolution, they develop a more nuanced appreciation of the story. This analytical approach enables them to engage with the text more profoundly, drawing connections between the author's intent and the narrative execution.

Moreover, acknowledging how themes drive the plot can illuminate character development. Characters are not static entities; they evolve in response to the thematic forces that shape their worlds. Consider J.K. Rowling's *Harry Potter* series, where the theme of love's power to overcome evil is intricately linked to Harry's growth. His relationships with friends and mentors, as well as his confrontations with Voldemort, are all influenced by this central theme, which ultimately defines his heroic journey.

Foreshadowing as a technique also enhances the reader's thematic experience. When authors plant seeds early in the story, they create a sense of anticipation and coherence. In F. Scott Fitzgerald's *The Great Gatsby*, the green light at the end of Daisy's dock symbolises Gatsby's unattainable dreams and foreshadows the tragic unravelling of his aspirations. This seemingly minor detail gains profound significance as the plot unfolds, reinforcing the themes of yearning and the American Dream.

At the story's resolution, the thematic message often becomes unmistakably clear. This moment of revelation can be powerful and thought-provoking, prompting readers to reflect on the broader implications of the narrative. In John Steinbeck's *Of Mice and Men*, the resolution poignantly encapsulates the themes of friendship and the harsh realities of the American Dream. George's heartbreaking decision to kill Lennie is a culmination of their journey together, infused with the thematic weight of sacrifice and disillusionment.

By understanding how themes are woven into plot structures, readers can better appreciate the complexity and depth of literary works. This knowledge empowers them to engage in meaningful discussions about the texts they encounter, enhancing their ability to interpret and analyse literature. It also nurtures a more profound emotional connection to the stories, as the interplay between themes and plot structures brings to life the human experiences and societal issues that resonate across time and cultures.

What We Learnt

In this chapter, we delved into the concepts of themes and motifs in literature. We explored how themes represent the central messages or ideas authors wish to convey, while motifs are recurring elements that reinforce these themes throughout a narrative. By examining examples from various novels, such as the use of light and darkness in "Lord of the Flies" and the green light in "The Great Gatsby," we illustrated how identifying these elements can enrich our understanding of the text. Recognising themes and motifs enhances our appreciation of the author's craft and allows us to uncover deeper layers of meaning within a story.

As you continue your literary journey, remember that themes and motifs are tools authors use to communicate with readers on a profound level. They invite us to look beyond the surface and connect with the universal truths embedded in the narrative. Whether reading for pleasure or academic study, watching for these elements can transform your reading experience, making it more engaging and insightful. So, next time you pick up a novel, take a moment to reflect on the themes and motifs at play; you might be surprised by the depth and complexity you'll discover.

CHAPTER X

Point of View and Narrative Voice

"Point of view and narrative voice are crucial elements in storytelling that shape how readers perceive and connect with a story. By choosing the proper perspective, authors can control the flow of information and evoke specific emotions, guiding readers through the narrative journey. This chapter delves into various narrative styles, each offering distinct advantages and challenges for writers. Understanding these differences is essential for creating compelling and engaging stories."

This chapter explores several narrative techniques by examining first-person narration, third-person limited, and third-person omniscient perspectives. It will highlight how each style influences reader engagement and the plot's unfolding. Additionally, the chapter discusses unreliable narrators who add layers of complexity and intrigue to a story. Through detailed examples and analysis, this chapter aims to provide valuable insights for aspiring writers and keen readers looking to deepen their appreciation of literary craft.

First-person Narration

First-person narration is a powerful storytelling tool that can connect the narrator and reader intimately. By using 'I,' a first-person narrative allows readers to experience the story through the storyteller's thoughts, feelings, and perspectives. This technique draws readers closer, making them privy to the narrator's inner world and unique experiences, enhancing their emotional investment in the narrative.

One of the most compelling aspects of first-person narration is its ability to reveal the depth of a character's psyche. As readers are presented with the direct thoughts and feelings of the narrator, they gain insight into motivations, fears, hopes, and desires that might otherwise remain hidden. This level of intimacy can make readers feel as though they are living the story alongside the narrator, blurring the lines between fiction and reality. This perspective can also heighten the tension and suspense, as readers are limited to what the narrator knows and perceives, often leading to unexpected twists and turns.

For instance, consider using first-person narration in J.D. Salinger's "The Catcher in the Rye." Through the character of Holden Caulfield, readers are drawn into his tumultuous adolescence, experiencing his confusion, angst, and disillusionment firsthand. Holden's candid, often unreliable account of events creates a vivid, relatable portrait of a teenager grappling with complex emotions and societal expectations. Similarly, Sylvia Plath's "The Bell Jar" uses first-person narration to depict Esther Greenwood's descent into mental illness, offering an unflinchingly honest portrayal of her struggle with identity and depression. These examples demonstrate how first-person narration can foster empathy by illuminating the narrator's innermost conflicts and vulnerabilities.

However, first-person narration does not merely convey emotion; it can also shape a reader's perception and bias. Since the story is filtered through the narrator's lens, their opinions, prejudices, and interpretations heavily influence how the narrative unfolds. This subjective viewpoint can lead readers to form specific allegiances or aversions based on the narrator's depiction of events and characters. For example, in Charlotte Brontë's "Jane Eyre," Jane's perspective invites readers to sympathise with her plight and see other characters, such as Mr. Rochester, through her eyes. This manipulation of reader bias underscores the power of first-person narration to create a personalised reading experience, where individual interpretation plays a significant role in engagement and understanding.

While first-person narration's intimacy and emotional resonance are undeniable strengths, this narrative style also presents particular challenges. One major limitation is the difficulty in presenting multiple viewpoints. Because the story is confined to the narrator's perspective, providing a balanced view or exploring other characters' experiences in depth can be challenging. This focus on a single viewpoint may result in a narrow or biased portrayal of events, leaving readers with an incomplete picture of the story's broader context.

Additionally, there is the risk of over-identification with the narrator. When readers closely align themselves with the narrator's perspective, they may become less critical of the narrator's actions and judgments, potentially skewing their overall interpretation of the narrative. This issue is particularly pertinent in cases where the narrator is unreliable or flawed, as readers may struggle to discern objective truth from subjective perception. Authors must navigate this terrain carefully, ensuring the narrator's voice remains compelling while allowing readers to question and reflect on their reliability.

Despite these challenges, first-person narration remains a popular and effective storytelling device that can deeply engage readers through its immersive, personal approach.

Providing direct access to a character's inner world fosters a sense of closeness and empathy, drawing readers into the story's fabric. While it requires careful handling to balance subjectivity and maintain narrative coherence, when executed well, first-person narration has the potential to elevate the reading experience, making it both captivating and thought-provoking.

Third-person Limited vs. Omniscient

Understanding the nuances between third-person limited and omniscient perspectives is fundamental for anyone delving into narrative storytelling. Each perspective offers distinct methods for guiding readers through a story, shaping their emotional experiences, and providing varying depths of understanding about characters and events.

Third-person limited perspective focuses on one character's viewpoint at a time, immersing the reader deeply in that character's thoughts, feelings, and sensory experiences. This perspective allows for an intimate exploration of a single character's inner world, making it easier for readers to connect with and understand the character's motivations and emotions. For example, in J.K. Rowling's *Harry Potter* series, much of the narrative is presented from Harry's point of view, allowing readers to follow his journey, struggles, and triumphs closely. By limiting the perspective, this style can create suspense and tension, as readers are only privy to the knowledge and perceptions of one character, experiencing discoveries and surprises right along with them.

On the other hand, the third-person omniscient perspective provides an all-knowing narrator with access to multiple characters' thoughts, feelings, and experiences. This broader viewpoint can offer a more comprehensive understanding of the story's universe. Classic literature such as Leo Tolstoy's *War and Peace* employs this method, revealing the intricacies of numerous lives against the backdrop of historical events. Through the omniscient viewpoint, readers gain insights into various characters' inner workings, motivations, and interconnections, which can enhance the richness and complexity of the narrative.

The choice between third-person limited and omniscient perspectives significantly impacts storytelling. Third-person limited perspectives can foster a deeper emotional connection with the protagonist, drawing readers into their journey. They often result in a more focused and intense narrative, where the character's subjective experiences shape the reader's perception of the story world. However, this limitation can sometimes feel restrictive if the reader desires a broader understanding of the context or other characters' motives.

Conversely, third-person omniscient offers the flexibility to move across different characters and settings, presenting a multi-faceted narrative view. This can enrich the story by illustrating how characters' lives intertwine and influence each other. However, there is a risk that the frequent shifts in perspective might dilute the reader's emotional engagement with any single character, potentially leading to a less immersive experience.

When examining the strengths and weaknesses of both perspectives, it's clear that authors must carefully consider their storytelling goals. Third-person limited excels in creating deep, personal connections with characters, making it ideal for stories that revolve around individual growth and internal conflict. An example is George R.R. Martin's *A Song of Ice and Fire*, where chapters alternate between different characters' limited viewpoints, allowing readers to explore various facets of the complex narrative while maintaining intense personal insights.

In contrast, third-person omniscient shines in narratives that require a broad scope, encompassing multiple plotlines and character arcs. This perspective is efficient in epic tales that span significant periods or diverse locations. Another example is J.R.R. Tolkien's *The Lord of the Rings*, where the omniscient viewpoint enriches the expansive world-building and the intricate interplay between numerous characters and events.

Narrative transitions are crucial when blending these perspectives within a single story. Smoothly shifting between third-person limited and omniscient views can provide a dynamic reading experience without causing confusion or disconnection. One technique is to use clear chapter breaks or scene changes to signal a shift in perspective. This approach helps maintain a coherent narrative flow while offering varied insights. In Suzanne Collins's The Hunger Games, the narrative remains mostly within Katniss Everdeen's limited viewpoint but occasionally steps back to provide broader context, such as descriptions of the Capitol's reactions, thereby blending personal and broader perspectives effectively.

Another approach involves subtle narrative cues that guide the reader through transitions, such as tone, language or focus changes. For instance, transitioning from a character's inner thoughts to an external action or event can signal a shift from a limited to a more omniscient view. By balancing these shifts thoughtfully, authors can deepen readers' engagement and appreciation of the narrative's complexity.

Understanding and distinguishing between third-person limited and omniscient perspectives is essential for crafting compelling stories. Each perspective offers unique advantages: third-person limited for deep character exploration and emotional connection and third-person omniscient for a comprehensive, multifaceted narrative. By carefully considering their storytelling objectives and employing effective narrative transitions, writers can harness the strengths of both perspectives, enriching their tales and enhancing reader engagement.

Unreliable Narrators

To explore how unreliable narrators challenge readers to question truth and perception, we must first understand what an unreliable narrator is. An unreliable narrator is a character whose credibility has been compromised. This unreliability can stem from various factors, such as mental instability, intentional deceit, or a limited understanding of the events around them. Because of this, readers are often required to engage more actively with the text, constantly questioning what they are being told and striving to piece together the real story from the fragments provided.

When discussing types of unreliability, we can categorise them into different forms: philosophical, psychological, and intentional deception. Philosophical unreliability occurs when the narrator's worldview or belief system is fundamentally at odds with reality, as the general populace understands. For example, in some stories, a character might interpret ordinary events as supernatural because of their personal beliefs. Psychological unreliability, on the other hand, arises from a narrator's mental illness or instability. In such cases, hallucinations, delusions, or extreme emotions distort their version of events. Finally, intentional deception refers to narrators who knowingly lie or manipulate information for their purposes. This could be to save face, achieve a specific goal, or simply because they derive pleasure from misleading others.

One classic example of an unreliable narrator is Agatha Christie's "The Murder of Roger Ackroyd," where Dr. Sheppard conceals crucial information until the end, leading readers down a false path. This deliberate omission creates a sense of betrayal and forces readers to reconsider everything they have read with a sceptical eye. Another notable instance is Patrick Bateman in Bret Easton Ellis' "American Psycho." Bateman's graphic recounting of his violent acts makes readers question the line between reality and his psychotic delusions. These case studies illustrate how unreliable narrators can employ techniques such as embellishment, omission of details, or outright lies to manipulate the narrative.

Unreliable narrators create a distinctive reading experience by exploring the impact on reader engagement. They encourage readers to become detectives, piecing together clues and questioning each story element. This active participation deepens engagement, making the narrative more interactive and immersive. Furthermore, the uncertainty introduced by an unreliable narrator can fuel critical thinking, prompting readers to analyse and debate the true meaning behind the text. It also invites repeated readings, as individuals often revisit the story to uncover new layers of understanding or catch previously missed hints.

Multiple Perspectives

One of the most compelling techniques in narrative storytelling is the use of multiple perspectives. This approach allows readers to dive into the minds and experiences of various characters, offering a richer, more complex understanding of the story. By presenting different viewpoints, authors can create deep and multifaceted narratives.

To begin with, let's delve into what multiple perspectives entail. In literature, this technique involves telling the story through the eyes of several characters rather than just one. Each character's perspective adds a unique layer to the narrative, revealing personal thoughts, emotions, and motivations that may not be apparent from a single viewpoint. This method helps create a multi-dimensional picture, encouraging readers to see events from various angles and better understand the complexities within the story.

The benefits of employing multiple perspectives are numerous. Firstly, it broadens the reader's comprehension of the narrative. When a story is told through different lenses, it becomes easier for readers to grasp the full scope of events and their impact on each character. For instance, a conflict seen through the eyes of the protagonist and antagonist provides insight into their differing motivations, leading to a more balanced and empathetic view of the situation. This, in turn, fosters greater emotional engagement as readers become more invested in the characters' journeys and the overall plot.

Additionally, multiple perspectives enrich the story by adding depth and complexity. Stories with a singular viewpoint can sometimes feel limited or one-dimensional. However, when multiple characters share their experiences, the narrative gains layers of intrigue and nuance. Readers enjoy piecing together the various accounts, uncovering hidden connections and themes that might go unnoticed. This layered storytelling keeps readers hooked as they eagerly anticipate new revelations and insights from each character's point of view.

Many notable novels effectively use multiple perspectives to enhance their narratives. A prime example is "As I Lay Dying" by William Faulkner. Fifteen characters narrate this novel, each providing their account of the journey to bury their deceased mother. Through these varied perspectives, Faulkner creates a rich tapestry of familial relationships, personal struggles, and regional culture. The diversity of voices gives readers a comprehensive understanding of the character's inner lives and the broader context of their actions.

Another excellent example is "Cloud Atlas" by David Mitchell. This ambitious novel weaves together six stories set across various periods and locations, each narrated by a different character. As readers move through the book, they discover intricate links between the characters and their narratives, highlighting the interconnectedness of human experiences across time and space. Mitchell's use of multiple perspectives not only enhances the thematic depth of the novel but also provides a captivating reading experience.

Several practical techniques exist for writers interested in incorporating multiple perspectives into their work. One key strategy is ensuring that each character's voice remains distinct. This can be achieved through careful attention to language, tone, and style. For instance, a teenage narrator might use informal, colloquial speech, while an older character might have a more formal, reflective tone. These differences help readers distinguish between perspectives and authenticate each character's portrayal.

Another essential technique is managing the transitions between viewpoints. Smooth, clear transitions are vital to maintaining the flow of the narrative and preventing reader confusion. Some authors use chapter breaks or section headings to signal shifts in perspective, making it easy for readers to follow along. Others might employ subtle changes in the writing style or use visual cues like paragraph breaks. Whatever method is chosen, the goal is to guide the reader effortlessly from one viewpoint to another without disrupting the story's momentum.

It's also crucial for writers to balance the attention given to each perspective. Over-focusing on one character can make others feel underdeveloped, diminishing the overall impact of the multiple viewpoints. By evenly distributing the narrative focus, authors ensure that each character's story is sufficiently explored and contributes meaningfully to the overarching plot. This balance keeps the narrative dynamic and ensures every voice adds value to the reader's understanding.

Additionally, writers should be mindful of how the different perspectives interact and contrast. Highlighting conflicts and agreements between characters' viewpoints can add tension and drama to the story. For example, two characters might interpret the same event differently, sparking a conflict that propels the narrative forward. On the other hand, aligning perspectives can reinforce themes and deepen the reader's connection to the characters. These harmonious or contentious interactions are essential for creating a cohesive and engaging narrative.

What We Learnt

In exploring the various narrative perspectives in this chapter, we've delved into how different narrations shape the storytelling experience. Through first-person narration, we see how the intimacy of a single viewpoint can draw readers closer to the narrator's inner world, enhancing emotional engagement and creating a personalised reading journey. The limitations of this perspective also highlight the challenges of presenting a balanced view, often leading to a skewed interpretation based on the narrator's biases. In contrast, the third-person perspectives, both limited and omniscient, offer unique advantages in guiding readers through the narrative, whether by focusing intensely on one character or providing a broader understanding of multiple characters and their interconnections.

Examining unreliable narrators introduced us to the complexities they bring to storytelling, challenging readers to question truths and piece together hidden realities. Such narrators add depth and intrigue, making the reading experience more interactive. Additionally, multiple perspectives offer a multifaceted view of events, enriching the story and deepening our connection with each character's journey. By employing these storytelling techniques thoughtfully, writers can create engaging and thought-provoking narratives that captivate readers from beginning to end.

CHAPTER XI

A Study of Novel Types

"Exploring the vast world of novel genres can be both exciting and enlightening. The literature landscape is rich with diverse genres, each with its characteristics defining the storytelling approach, the themes explored, and the emotional experiences they evoke. Understanding these distinctive features helps readers appreciate how different styles and themes shape narratives, creating unique reading experiences."

This chapter will delve into various novel genres to uncover what makes each one special. From the detailed depictions of everyday life in realism and naturalism to the eerie gothic and horror fiction atmospheres, we'll examine how authors use different techniques to build their worlds and convey their messages. You will learn about the common themes in these genres and see examples from influential works that have shaped literature. By the end of this chapter, you'll have a deeper understanding of how genre influences storytelling and the varied ways authors draw us into their narratives.

Realism and Naturalism

Realism and naturalism are two significant movements in literature aiming to reflect the real world accurately. Both emphasise the depiction of everyday life and social conditions, providing readers with a mirror of their experiences and social environment. However, they differ subtly yet notably in their scope and focus.

Realism is a literary movement that strives to represent life as it is. It avoids idealisation and romanticised portrayals, focusing on ordinary people and their everyday activities. Realist writers delve into the mundane details of life, often highlighting the societal structures and class distinctions that define human existence. By doing so, they present a truthful, unembellished view of the world. The goal is to depict characters, events, and settings as realistically as possible, ensuring the reader can relate to the story and its context.

One prominent example that illustrates the principles of realism is Gustave Flaubert's "Madame Bovary." In this novel, Flaubert meticulously details the life of Emma Bovary, a doctor's wife who becomes disillusioned with her provincial life. Through Emma's struggles with her desires and the constraints of society, Flaubert exposes the harsh realities faced by individuals trapped in unfulfilling lives. His detailed descriptions of the setting and characters create a vivid picture that immerses the reader in the world he depicts. Flaubert's attention to detail and focus on his characters' inner lives exemplify the core tenets of realism.

Naturalism extends beyond realism by emphasising the influence of the environment and heredity on human behaviour. Naturalist writers often explore how external forces, such as social conditions, environment, and genetics, shape individuals' actions and destinies. In this sense, naturalism introduces a more scientific approach to literature, seeking to explain human behaviour through the lens of natural forces. Characters in naturalist works are often depicted as being at the mercy of forces beyond their control, which adds a deterministic element to the narratives.

Émile Zola is a crucial figure in the naturalist movement. His novel Germinal provides an in-depth exploration of the lives of coal miners in 19th-century France. Zola's portrayal of the harsh working conditions, poverty, and oppressive social structure underscores the impact of environment and heredity on the characters. The novel reveals how these factors drive the miners towards rebellion and highlight the inevitable struggles between different social classes. Zola's work captures not only individual suffering but also the collective experience of a community shaped by its environment.

Common themes in realism and naturalism include social class, moral dilemmas, and the human struggle. These themes encourage readers to reflect deeply on human behaviour and societal norms. Literature from these movements often focuses on the challenges faced by individuals and communities, prompting readers to consider the complexities of life and the various factors influencing people's decisions and outcomes.

In both realism and naturalism, social class is a critical theme. Realist and naturalist authors often depict the lives of lower and middle-class individuals, offering a critique of the societal structures that perpetuate inequality. For instance, in "Madame Bovary," Emma's dissatisfaction stems partly from her social status, which limits her opportunities and fuels her longing for a more glamorous life. Similarly, in "Germinal," the miners' plight is directly linked to the rigid class system that exploits their labour and keeps them impoverished. By highlighting these issues, authors raise awareness about the social injustices of their time and invite readers to question the fairness of the existing social order.

Moral dilemmas also feature prominently in realist and naturalist works. Characters are often placed in situations where they must make difficult choices, revealing their moral complexities and the conflicts between personal desires and societal expectations. These dilemmas add depth to the characters and make them more relatable to readers. In "Madame Bovary," Emma's extramarital affairs and financial irresponsibility lead to her downfall, illustrating the consequences of her attempts to escape her mundane existence. Her actions provoke sympathy and judgment, prompting readers to consider their moral beliefs and the pressures that influence human behaviour.

The human struggle, another common theme, encompasses individuals' daily battles, whether against societal norms, personal limitations, or environmental conditions. This theme resonates strongly with readers because it reflects universal experiences. Through their exploration of human struggles, realist and naturalist authors provide insight into the resilience and vulnerabilities of the human spirit. In "Germinal," the miners' fight for better working conditions and their ultimate revolt symbolise the human struggle for dignity and justice. Their perseverance despite overwhelming odds highlights the enduring nature of the human quest for a better life.

Seminal works like "Madame Bovary" and "Germinal" serve as case studies for understanding genre conventions and emotional engagement. These novels adhere to the principles of realism and naturalism and evoke strong emotional responses from readers. Flaubert's and Zola's detailed characterisations and vivid depictions of social conditions draw readers into the narrative, allowing them to empathise with the characters' experiences.

Gothic and Horror Fiction

Gothic and horror fiction have long captivated readers with their ability to evoke deep-seated fears and dark curiosity. While closely related, these genres possess distinct characteristics that uniquely shape their narratives. Understanding these elements can enrich our appreciation of how they play on emotional and psychological levels.

At the heart of gothic fiction lies an eerie atmosphere designed to evoke fear and stir the imagination. Settings such as decaying castles, haunted mansions, and desolate landscapes commonly create an unsettling backdrop. These environments are not merely passive settings but active participants in the story, influencing the mood and actions of characters. Gothic fiction often features complex, multi-faceted characters who grapple with internal conflicts and moral ambiguities. The supernatural plays a significant role, blurring the lines between reality and fantasy and enhancing the sense of dread.

On the other hand, horror fiction amplifies these gothic elements to instil pure terror. While gothic tales may focus more on slow-burning suspense, horror stories aim for immediate and intense reactions from readers. This genre employs graphic depictions of violence, grotesque imagery, and shock value to jolt the audience. The primary objective is to confront readers with their deepest fears and provoke visceral responses that linger long after the last page is turned.

Themes such as isolation, madness, and the uncanny are central to both genres, providing a lens through which we can explore the human psyche's darker corners. Physical or emotional isolation creates a fertile ground for fear to grow. Characters trapped in lonely, remote places or cut off from society face inner demons and external threats alike. Madness often blurs the boundary between sanity and insanity, casting doubt on what is real and what is imagined. The uncanny—where something familiar becomes terrifyingly strange—adds another layer of psychological complexity, deeply unsettling ordinary objects or occurrences.

Prominent authors like Mary Shelley and Edgar Allan Poe have significantly shaped gothic and horror literature. Mary Shelley's "Frankenstein" masterfully combines gothic elements with a cautionary tale about unchecked ambition and the perils of playing god. The novel's isolated setting, monstrous creation, and tragic hero contribute to its enduring power and influence. Meanwhile, Edgar Allan Poe's works, such as "The Tell-Tale Heart" and "The Fall of the House of Usher," delve into madness, guilt, and decay themes. Poe's innovative narrative techniques, including unreliable narrators and intricate plots, have left an indelible mark on the genre.

These historical figures set the stage for future generations, yet modern authors continue to breathe new life into gothic horror. Contemporary writers reimagine these genres to reflect current societal issues, expanding their relevance. They tackle themes like technological anxiety, environmental collapse, and systemic oppression within the framework of gothic horror. This evolution allows the genre to remain fresh and engaging, inspiring new writers to explore their creative boundaries.

For instance, contemporary novels like Shirley Jackson's "The Haunting of Hill House" and Stephen King's "The Shining" blend traditional gothic elements with modern themes. Jackson's work explores psychological distress and the haunted mind, while King examines family dynamics and personal failure within supernatural horror. Both authors push the envelope, proving that gothic horror can address contemporary concerns as effectively as it can entertain.

In addition, modern interpretations often feature diverse voices and perspectives, offering a richer tapestry of experiences and emotions. Authors such as Marlon James and Silvia Moreno-Garcia infuse their cultural backgrounds into gothic narratives, creating unique and haunting stories that resonate on multiple levels. By incorporating elements of their heritage and addressing timely social issues, they open up new avenues for exploring fear and human nature.

Historical Novels

Historical novels engage readers in specific periods, weaving research with storytelling to educate and reflect on history's impact on identity and societal norms. These novels delicately transport readers to bygone eras while maintaining relevance to contemporary issues. Readers understand how past events have shaped present-day society and cultural identities by immersing themselves in different historical contexts.

To achieve this vivid depiction of history, authors of historical novels invest significant effort into researching the periods they write about. This involves delving into primary sources like letters, diaries, and official documents and secondary sources such as academic studies and historical analyses. This meticulous research allows authors to create rich, immersive worlds that accurately reflect the social, political, and economic conditions of the times they portray. For example, Hilary Mantel's "Wolf Hall" series is renowned for its detailed depiction of Tudor England, where she brings courtly intrigue and the complex character of Thomas Cromwell to life.

Mantel's work exemplifies how historical novels can blend fact with fiction. While the overarching narrative may be rooted in historical events, authors often introduce fictional elements to fill in gaps or enhance the story's emotional depth. In doing so, they create a narrative that feels authentic and engaging, helping readers connect with the characters and events. Similarly, Ken Follett's "The Pillars of the Earth" explores the construction of a cathedral in medieval England, interweaving the struggles and triumphs of fictional characters with actual historical events and figures, such as Thomas Becket.

Historical novels frequently feature themes of power, betrayal, and cultural conflicts, challenging readers to consider diverse historical perspectives and lessons. Power dynamics often take centre stage as these novels explore how individuals and groups vie for control and influence within their societies. Betrayal is another common theme, reflecting the personal and political intrigues that shape human history. Cultural conflicts, whether between different social classes, religions, or ethnic groups, underscore the complexities of historical change and continuity.

For instance, in Mantel's "Bring Up the Bodies," the themes of power and betrayal are intertwined as Thomas Cromwell navigates the treacherous waters of Henry VIII's court. The novel reveals the precarious nature of political alliances and the lengths individuals will go to secure their positions of power. Similarly, in Follett's "World Without End," set in the same fictional town of Kingsbridge two centuries after "The Pillars of the Earth," readers encounter themes of social upheaval and conflict as the Black Death ravages Europe. The novel examines how communities grapple with crisis, highlighting human societies' resilience and vulnerability.

These themes provide compelling narratives and prompt readers to reflect on their experiences and world. The authors offer insights into the complexities of human behaviour and societal development by presenting historical conflicts and resolutions. Through the lens of the past, readers can better understand contemporary issues and appreciate the enduring relevance of historical events.

Historical novels also serve as a bridge to understanding current events, fostering connections across generations and providing tools for analysing past conflicts. Drawing parallels between historical and modern situations, these novels encourage readers to consider how historical patterns and decisions continue to influence the present. For example, in Colson Whitehead's "The Underground Railroad," the brutal realities of slavery and the journey toward freedom resonate with ongoing discussions about racial injustice and inequality in today's society.

Moreover, historical novels can inspire readers to see history as an active and dynamic field rather than a static collection of facts. They emphasise the importance of historical consciousness—an awareness of how the past shapes the present and future. Through engaging storytelling, these novels make history accessible and relevant, particularly to younger audiences who might otherwise find historical study dry or disconnected from their lives.

In addition, historical novels often highlight lesser-known aspects of history, bringing marginalised voices and overlooked events to the forefront. This inclusive approach broadens readers' understanding of history and acknowledges the contributions of diverse groups. For instance, Chimamanda Ngozi Adichie's "Half of a Yellow

Sun" sheds light on the Nigerian Civil War, which is not widely covered in mainstream historical narratives. Through her compelling characters and vivid descriptions, Adichie gives readers a deeper understanding of the war's impact on Nigeria and its people.

Speculative Fiction (Sci-Fi, Fantasy)

Speculative fiction engages the imagination, transcending the boundaries of reality to explore future possibilities and fantastical realms. It encompasses subgenres like science fiction and fantasy, but at its core, it aims to challenge our understanding of the world. By juxtaposing elements of the unknown with our tangible realities, speculative fiction creates a playground for ideas that reflect real-life issues.

One of the most fascinating aspects of speculative fiction is its emphasis on world-building and imaginative explorations. This genre allows authors to construct unique worlds with intricate details, offering readers an escape into realms where anything is possible. For instance, in J.R.R. Tolkien's Middle-earth, readers are transported to a meticulously crafted universe filled with diverse races, languages, and histories. Similarly, Isaac Asimov's "Foundation" series constructs a futuristic society governed by complex scientific principles. Through these immersive settings, speculative fiction mirrors our world and sheds light on contemporary societal issues. Whether exploring the consequences of technological advancements or highlighting social inequalities, the genre uses fantastical backdrops to question and critique our reality.

Influenced authors like Isaac Asimov and J.R.R. Tolkien are central to speculative fiction, whose works have defined and shaped the genre. With his profound understanding of science and technology, Asimov delves into themes such as artificial intelligence, ethics, and the future of humanity. His work challenges readers to consider the ethical implications of scientific progress and the role of humans in an increasingly technologically driven world. On the other hand, Tolkien's contribution to fantasy literature is unparalleled. His attention to detail in creating mythologies, cultures, and languages enriches his narratives, allowing readers to fully immerse themselves in his characters' fantastical yet relatable struggles. These authors' abilities to blend imaginative world-building with complex themes set a high standard for the genre, influencing countless writers and readers.

A key aspect of speculative fiction is its exploration of familiar themes such as technology, ethics, and humanity. These themes serve as a conduit for readers to question their surroundings and assumptions. For example, dystopian science fiction often explores the potential pitfalls of technological advancements. George Orwell's "1984," for example, warns of the dangers of a surveillance state and the loss of individual freedoms. At the same time, it sparks discussions about the ethical use of technology and the balance between security and privacy. In fantasy literature, themes of humanity and ethics are explored through allegorical tales. Characters confront moral dilemmas and embark on journeys that reflect our struggles, encouraging readers to ponder what it means to be human and how we should navigate our ethical choices. The intersection of these themes in speculative fiction fosters a space for innovation and societal reflection.

In recent years, contemporary speculative fiction has made significant strides in incorporating diverse voices, expanding the genre to reflect broader identities and cultures. This inclusivity enriches the genre, bringing fresh perspectives and new narratives that resonate with a wider audience—authors such as N.K. Jemisin and Liu Cixin have introduced readers to worlds influenced by varied cultural backgrounds and experiences. Jemisin's "Broken Earth" trilogy, for instance, presents a world shaped by geological upheaval while addressing themes of oppression and resilience. Her narrative draws from her African-American heritage, adding depth and authenticity to her storytelling. Similarly, Liu Cixin's "The Three-Body Problem" trilogy brings Chinese culture and history into the speculative fiction landscape, offering a unique perspective on humanity's place in the cosmos. These diverse voices not only broaden the scope of speculative fiction but also inspire dialogues about representation and inclusion, encouraging readers to see the world through different lenses.

Incorporating diverse voices in speculative fiction also means addressing underrepresented groups and challenging traditional tropes. By doing so, the genre becomes a platform for marginalised perspectives, fostering empathy and understanding among readers. Works that highlight LGBTQ+ characters, people of colour, and other underrepresented communities enrich the genre and push the boundaries of what speculative fiction can achieve. For example, Rivers Solomon's "An Unkindness of Ghosts" is a powerful exploration of race, gender, and identity within the confines of a generation starship. Solomon's work challenges readers to confront uncomfortable truths about discrimination and privilege, all while delivering a compelling narrative. By embracing diversity, contemporary speculative fiction remains relevant and paves the way for more inclusive and representative storytelling.

Speculative fiction bridges the imaginable and the unimaginable, inviting readers to explore worlds beyond their own while contemplating pressing societal issues. Its ability to speculate on future possibilities, delve into fantastical realms and challenge our perceptions makes it a valuable genre for entertainment and intellectual stimulation. As students, educators, and young adult readers engage with this genre, they gain a deeper appreciation for the power of imagination and its role in shaping our understanding of reality. By immersing themselves in the creative landscapes of speculative fiction, they learn to think critically, embrace diversity, and envision a future where innovation and empathy coexist.

What We Learnt

In this chapter, we've explored the distinct features of various novel genres, diving into realism and naturalism, gothic and horror fiction, historical novels, and speculative fiction. We examined how each genre creates unique worlds and experiences for readers while tackling themes such as social class, moral dilemmas, human struggles, fear, power dynamics, cultural conflicts, technology, ethics, and humanity. By understanding these elements, we gain insights into how different styles and themes shape narratives in literature, helping us deepen our appreciation and analytical skills.

Whether we're transported to the gritty realism of "Madame Bovary," the chilling atmosphere of Poe's tales, the richly detailed world of Tudor England, or the imaginative realms of Tolkien, each genre offers something unique. Literature becomes a mirror reflecting societal norms and individual behaviours, inviting us to ponder our own lives and the broader human experience. This chapter encourages young adult readers, students, and educators alike to embrace the diversity of literary genres, enhancing their reading enjoyment and ability to engage deeply with novels.

CHAPTER XII

Literary Analysis of the Novel

"Techniques for literary analysis can transform your reading experience, allowing you to appreciate novels more profoundly and insightfully. Engaging with a text using various analytical methods can turn any book into a treasure trove of meaning and interpretation. This chapter will uncover the tools that make literary analysis possible and enjoyable. Whether you're an avid reader or someone diving into literature for academic purposes, mastering these techniques will enhance your understanding of the stories you read and their layers."

This chapter will guide you through several critical methods for dissecting and engaging with novels. First, we'll explore how active reading strategies can help you interact more deeply with the text. Then, we'll identify narrative structures and understand different storytelling methods. We'll also examine characterisation, examining how characters drive plots and embody themes. Lastly, we'll discuss the importance of recognising literary devices such as symbolism, irony, and foreshadowing. By equipping yourself with these techniques, you'll be prepared to engage with literature on a deeper level, enriching your appreciation and comprehension of the works you study.

Critical Reading Strategies

Enhancing critical reading skills is essential for students and literature enthusiasts aiming to delve deeper into novels. Readers can enrich their understanding and appreciation of literary works by employing active reading techniques, identifying narrative structures, engaging with characterisation, and recognising literary devices.

Active reading is a foundational strategy that transforms the passive consumption of text into an interactive experience. Engaging with the text through annotations allows readers to track significant points, reactions, and questions directly on the page. This helps maintain focus and retain information. For example, highlighting key sentences or important phrases can serve as quick reference points when reviewing the text later and prompting students to ask questions while reading is crucial. Questions such as "Why did the author choose this particular setting?" or "What motivates this character's actions?" stimulate critical thinking and deeper engagement with the content. Such questioning develops a critical mindset and enables readers to anticipate plot developments and understand character motivations more thoroughly.

Another effective method is summarising critical points at the end of each chapter or section. By writing summaries, readers reinforce their comprehension and reflect on significant themes and events. This practice aids in retaining core ideas long after the initial reading. Encouraging note-taking throughout this process supports retention and allows more accessible review before discussions or exams.

Identifying narrative techniques is another crucial skill. Understanding how different storytelling methods impact the reader's perception and interpretation can significantly enhance analytical abilities. For instance, analysing first-person versus third-person narratives helps elucidate the author's intent and audience engagement. A first-person narrative might offer intimate insights into a character's inner world, fostering a personal connection with the reader. In contrast, a third-person narrative often provides a broader perspective, allowing readers to understand multiple characters and overarching plotlines simultaneously.

Examining the structure of the narrative also reveals much about the pacing and progression of the story. Flashbacks, nonlinear timelines, and different points of view contribute to the complexity of the narrative, creating layers of meaning that can be unpacked through analysis. Understanding why an author might choose to reveal certain information at specific points helps in comprehending the overall message and themes of the work.

Engaging deeply with characterisation involves comparing and contrasting characters to uncover core conflicts and themes within the novel. Characters drive the plot and embody the story's themes, making them central to any literary analysis. Readers can identify the narrative's fundamental conflict by analysing protagonists and antagonists. For instance, examining the moral complexities of characters like Jane Eyre or Captain Ahab in classic literature offers insight into human nature and societal norms.

Contrasting characters can also highlight differing worldviews or ethical dilemmas in the novel. Comparing characters' decisions and growth throughout the story sheds light on the author's underlying messages. This approach not only aids in understanding the characters themselves but also provides a comprehensive view of the narrative arc and thematic exploration.

Recognising literary devices is integral to appreciating the depth and artistry of a novel. Devices such as symbolism, irony, and foreshadowing are tools authors use to convey deeper meanings and enhance their storytelling. Symbolism, for instance, imbues objects, characters, or settings with additional layers of meaning beyond their literal sense. Analysing symbols within a text can unveil hidden themes and prompt reflections on broader social or psychological issues. For example, in F. Scott Fitzgerald's "The Great Gatsby," the green light symbolises Gatsby's unattainable dreams and the overarching theme of the American Dream's decay.

Irony, another potent literary device, often highlights discrepancies between appearance and reality, intention and outcome. Recognising ironic elements within a story encourages readers to question assumptions and explore the subtleties of the narrative. This critical approach allows for a multifaceted understanding of complex texts.

Authors use foreshadowing to hint at future events, building anticipation and enhancing the reader's engagement with the plot. Identifying instances of foreshadowing requires attentive reading and reflection on earlier text sections. As readers piece together clues leading to the climax, they foster a deepened connection with the storyline.

Character and Thematic Analysis

Analysing character development and thematic elements is crucial for delving deeper into any literary work. It allows readers to appreciate the narrative more nuancedly and helps them understand its broader implications.

To begin with, using a character analysis framework can significantly aid in visualising connections and transformations throughout a narrative. One effective tool is the character map. This visual representation tracks the characters' relationships and changes from the beginning to the end of the story. For example, in "To Kill a Mockingbird," a character map could help trace Scout Finch's growth from innocence to a more mature understanding of her community's complexities. By noting the interactions and critical events that shape her worldview, readers can better grasp how experiences influence character evolution.

Another essential aspect is thematic exploration. Identifying key themes involves recognising recurring ideas or messages that resonate throughout the novel. Themes often reflect universal human experiences and societal issues, allowing readers to connect them with their lives. In George Orwell's "1984," themes such as surveillance, totalitarianism, and individuality provide a lens through which readers can examine contemporary societal issues. Recognising these themes enhances comprehension and appreciation as readers see how literature mirrors and critiques real-world scenarios.

Contextual influences are equally crucial in literary analysis. Understanding the author's background can illuminate why certain characters are crafted in specific ways. For instance, knowing that Mary Shelley wrote "Frankenstein" during the Romantic era, an age fascinated by nature, science, and the sublime, enriches our understanding of Victor Frankenstein and his monstrous creation. Shelley's personal experiences and historical context influence the characters' motivations and actions, offering more profound insight into the narrative.

Exploring character relationships further strengthens this analysis. Characters do not exist in isolation; their interactions often drive the plot and reveal the central messages of the novel. For instance, in Jane Austen's "Pride and Prejudice," the evolving relationship between Elizabeth Bennet and Mr. Darcy underscores themes of social class, misunderstandings, and personal growth. By examining how their interactions change from initial prejudice to mutual respect, readers gain a deeper understanding of the novel's critical commentary on societal norms and individual transformation.

A comprehensive approach to character analysis involves synthesising all these elements. Begin by creating a character map to visualise connections and transformations. This helps organise thoughts and identify key moments that define characters' arcs. Next, delve into thematic exploration, linking identified themes to personal and societal narratives. Contextual influences provide another layer of depth, revealing how the author's life and times shape the story. Finally, scrutinise character relationships to uncover how they drive the plot and highlight inherent themes.

Engaging with these elements provides a structured methodology for literary analysis, making it accessible for both students and educators. For example, high school and college students will find this approach helpful in dissecting complicated texts, fostering a more profound understanding of literature. This structured framework allows them to write more insightful essays and participate in meaningful discussions.

This framework offers English teachers and educators a practical guide for teaching literary analysis. By guiding students through each element—character maps, thematic exploration, contextual influences, and character relationships—they can foster a classroom environment where students actively engage with the text. Discussing diverse perspectives and interpretations can enhance critical thinking and empathy among students, enriching their overall learning experience.

Young adult readers curious about literary analysis can use this method to elevate their reading enjoyment. By engaging with characters and themes, they can appreciate literature beyond surface-level enjoyment. This analytical approach encourages them to think critically about what they read, enabling more informed and articulate discussions about their favourite novels.

In summary, analysing character development and thematic elements requires a multifaceted approach. Utilise a character map to visualise connections and transformations, helping organise thoughts and identify fundamental narrative shifts. Explore critical themes to connect personal experiences with broader societal narratives, enriching comprehension and appreciation. Investigate contextual influences to understand how the author's background shapes the story, offering more profound insight into the characters' motivations and actions. Lastly, examine character relationships to reveal how they drive the plot and underscore central themes. This structured approach fosters a more profound engagement with literature, enhancing the reading experience for students, educators, and young adults.

Contextual and Intertextual Analysis

Exploring connections between a novel and its historical, cultural, and literary contexts is crucial for any comprehensive scholarly analysis. Understanding the context in which a book was written can reveal layers of meaning that might otherwise remain hidden. For example, analysing the historical period during which the author wrote can offer invaluable insights into the characters' worldviews and challenges.

Imagine reading a novel set during World War II. Knowing the history of that time can help you understand why characters behave in specific ways, what motivates them, or why they face particular dilemmas. This understanding bridges the gap between the fictional and real worlds, clarifying why the author made specific narrative choices. It's like peeling back layers of an onion; each layer reveals more about the plot, setting, and characters.

Next, intertextual connections can significantly enhance your appreciation of a novel. Intertextuality refers to how texts refer to and influence each other. Identifying references or allusions to other literature within a novel enriches your reading experience by adding depth and context. For instance, if a contemporary novel echoes themes from Shakespeare's works, recognising these allusions can deepen your understanding of the author's craft and intention.

Think about modern novels that reference mythology or classic literature. A character likened to Achilles from Greek mythology brings a wealth of pre-existing ideas and themes. Realising these connections enables readers to see beyond the surface story, appreciating the layers of meaning that make the work richer. This amplifies your engagement with the text and provides a broader perspective on the interconnectedness of literature over time.

Critical reception is another essential aspect to consider. Examining how critique evolves can offer a window into societal attitudes and how they affect the appreciation of literature. When a novel is first published, it may receive varied reviews depending on contemporary beliefs, cultural norms, and prevailing literary tastes. Over decades or even centuries, critical opinions can shift, sometimes dramatically.

Imagine a novel initially dismissed as trivial but later hailed as a masterpiece. Assessing changes in critical reception reveals shifts in literary taste and broader societal changes. For example, feminist readings of novels initially criticised for portraying women might later highlight those same aspects as groundbreaking. Understanding this evolution helps us grasp the ever-changing landscape of critical thought and its impact on literary appreciation.

Cultural impact is closely related to both historical context and critical reception. Analysing how a novel reflects and shapes cultural narratives can provide profound insights into its relevance and significance. Literature often does more than entertain; it can challenge societal norms, influence public opinion, and even drive social change. By assessing a novel's cultural impact, readers can appreciate its role in the broader social fabric.

Consider Harper Lee's "To Kill a Mockingbird." Its portrayal of racial injustice in the American South has had enduring cultural significance. The novel reflects the racial tensions of its time and has continued to influence discussions around race and justice. By understanding the cultural impact of such a work, readers gain a deeper appreciation of its relevance beyond the confines of its pages.

Interestingly, some novels have garnered a cultural legacy far exceeding their initial reception. J.D. Salinger's "The Catcher in the Rye" is a prime example. Initially controversial, it has become a staple in academic settings and a touchstone for generations of readers grappling with adolescence and identity. Its cultural influence is evident in various forms of media, resonating with themes of teenage rebellion and existential angst.

Examining these aspects—historical context, intertextual connections, critical reception, and cultural impact—provides a multifaceted approach to literary analysis. By dissecting these elements, readers can engage with novels on a much deeper level, appreciating not just the storyline but the intricate web of influences and implications that underpin the work.

This structured approach enhances comprehension and appreciation for high school and college students studying literature. Students can develop a nuanced view of any novel they read by exploring the historical background, understanding literary references, following the evolution of critiques, and assessing cultural impacts. This method makes literary analysis more accessible and engaging, making reading more interactive and enlightening experience.

English teachers and educators will also benefit from this approach, providing a practical framework for teaching students about novel study and critical analysis. Using these elements as focal points, they can guide students through the complexities of literary works, fostering greater engagement and understanding. Such a structured methodology ensures that critical thinking is applied consistently and effectively, promoting a deeper academic dialogue around literature.

Young adult readers, too, can find joy in approaching novels analytically. Understanding the myriad connections within a literary work can transform how they perceive books. It turns casual reading into a more rewarding endeavour, offering tools to discuss and critique literature more thoughtfully. Young adults can elevate their reading enjoyment and insight by delving into their novels' historical, cultural, and literary contexts.

Developing Thesis Statements

Crafting strong thesis statements is an essential skill for literary analysis. A well-written thesis statement is a roadmap for the entire essay, guiding readers through the arguments and ensuring a clear focus throughout the paper. It should be both clear and concise, encapsulating the main points the writer intends to argue.

Characteristics of Strong Thesis Statements

A robust thesis statement does more than state the topic of the essay; it also presents the writer's stance and provides insight into how the essay will be structured. First and foremost, clarity is critical. A reader should understand the central argument without re-reading the sentence multiple times. For example, instead of writing, "This essay discusses the themes in 'The Great Gatsby,'" a more precise and more focused thesis would be, "In 'The Great Gatsby,' F. Scott Fitzgerald critiques the American Dream by portraying its unattainability and the moral decay it brings." This specific thesis gives a clear direction for the essay, indicating that the writer will explore Fitzgerald's critique and its implications.

Conciseness is equally essential. A thesis statement that is too lengthy or filled with unnecessary jargon can confuse readers rather than guide them. Aim to express your main argument in one to two sentences. A concise thesis helps maintain reader interest and sets a strong foundation for the essay's body.

Linking Thesis to Textual Evidence

Once a strong thesis statement is crafted, the next step is to develop an analytical framework that effectively ties claims to textual support. This involves selecting relevant quotes, passages, or scenes from the novel that directly support the thesis. For instance, if your thesis argues that a character's evolution reflects broader societal changes, you must identify critical moments in the text where this transformation is evident.

Developing this framework starts with close reading. Highlight parts of the text that stand out, noting why they seem significant. Look for patterns, symbols, and motifs that align with your thesis. When incorporating these textual elements into your essay, explain how they support your argument. Don't just drop a quote and move on; take time to dissect it, showing its relevance to your thesis. You build a stronger, more persuasive argument by linking textual evidence to your thesis.

Revision Techniques

Creating a solid thesis statement often requires revision. Reflective revision promotes clearer argumentation and better alignment with textual evidence. Start by writing a draft of your thesis and then stepping back to review it critically. Ask yourself: Does this thesis answer a specific question about the text? Is it arguable, meaning someone could potentially disagree with it? Does it lay out a clear path for my essay?

One effective revision technique is peer review. Sharing your thesis with classmates or teachers can provide valuable feedback. They might point out areas of vagueness or suggest ways to make your argument more compelling. Reading your thesis aloud can also help you catch awkward phrasing or overly complex language.

Another helpful method is to revisit your thesis after drafting the body paragraphs. Sometimes, your argument evolves as you write, and your thesis may need adjustments to reflect these changes accurately. Don't hesitate to refine your thesis to ensure it remains aligned with the main arguments presented in your essay.

Thesis in Context of Broader Argument

Ensuring that your thesis statement aligns with the broader argument of your essay is crucial for maintaining coherence. Each paragraph should link back to the thesis, either supporting it directly or addressing potential counterarguments. This creates a unified narrative that guides the reader through your analysis seamlessly.

When structuring your essay, consider using topic sentences at the beginning of each paragraph that relate directly to your thesis. These sentences act as mini-theses, previewing the paragraph's discussion while tying it back to the overall argument. For example, suppose your thesis revolves around a character's journey. A topic sentence might be, "Gatsby's relentless pursuit of Daisy exemplifies his misguided belief in the attainability of the American Dream."

Additionally, transitions between paragraphs should reinforce the logical flow of your argument. Rather than jumping abruptly from one point to another, use transitional phrases to connect ideas smoothly. This not only enhances readability but also strengthens the cohesiveness of your essay.

Reflect on how your thesis fits within the larger context of literary studies. Consider how your argument contributes to existing interpretations of the text. Does it challenge conventional views? Does it offer a fresh perspective? You demonstrate a deeper engagement with the text and its critical interpretations by situating your thesis within the broader scholarly conversation.

What We Learnt

You now have a toolkit filled with strategies to deepen your literary analysis. From active reading and summarising critical points to recognising narrative techniques and character development, these methods empower you to engage with novels more profoundly. Each technique offers a unique lens through which to view the text, allowing you to uncover hidden themes and enhance your appreciation of the author's craft.

Remember, the goal is to make your reading experience interactive and reflective. As you apply these strategies, you'll find yourself asking more questions, making connections, and participating in richer discussions about literature. Whether a student, teacher or curious reader, embracing these approaches will transform your understanding of novels and elevate your critical reading skills.

Conclusion

"Why Study Novels? The Importance of Novels in Literature and Life

Novels have been an integral part of human culture and education for centuries. From the early epics and prose narratives to the diverse forms of novels we see today, they have captured the human experience, reflecting our dreams, struggles, emotions, and history. For students of literature and readers alike, studying novels is not just about reading stories; it explores art, society, psychology, and philosophy. Let's talk about why studying novels is academically and personally essential."

1. Understanding Human Experience

Novels have the transformative power to provide a deep insight into the human condition. Through the lives of fictional characters, readers can experience emotions, dilemmas, and struggles that may mirror their own or offer new perspectives on life. A well-written novel can allow readers to step into someone else's shoes and understand different ways of thinking, feeling, and living, inspiring them to broaden their horizons.

In *To Kill a Mockingbird* by Harper Lee, readers are exposed to issues of racial injustice, morality, and the innocence of childhood. The novel allows us to see the world through Scout Finch's eyes, a young girl growing up in the racially charged American South. By experiencing her perspective, readers empathise with others and are prompted to reflect on relevant moral issues.

Readers and students can broaden their perspectives by studying novels and accessing various human experiences. They can learn about cultures, emotions, and social issues they might not encounter daily, gaining a more comprehensive understanding of the world.

2. Enhancing Critical Thinking and Analysis

Studying novels is an excellent way to develop critical thinking skills. A story is more than just its plot; it is filled with symbols, themes, metaphors, and allegories that require deep analysis and interpretation. As readers, we are encouraged to look beyond the surface of the narrative and consider what the author might say about society, human nature, or politics.

George Orwell's **1984** is not just a story about a dystopian future but a profound commentary on totalitarian regimes, government surveillance, and the manipulation of truth. By studying this novel, students learn to analyse the political and philosophical messages embedded in the text, enhancing their ability to think critically about power structures and control in society.

Through the close study of novels, students learn to question and analyse texts, developing skills that can be applied to other academic disciplines and everyday life.

3. Cultural and Historical Insight

Novels often reflect the time in which they were written. They offer valuable insights into historical events, cultural practices, and societal values. By studying novels from different periods and regions, students can better understand the evolution of cultures, the impact of historical events, and how societal values have changed.

Charles Dickens's *A Tale of Two Cities* vividly portrays the French Revolution and its impact on French and English societies. The novel brings history to life, showing readers how events such as the revolution affected ordinary people. Students learn about the historical context by studying this novel and reflecting on themes of justice, sacrifice, and revolution.

Whether it's the Victorian era of Dickens, the Harlem Renaissance of Zora Neale Hurston, or the existentialism of Albert Camus, novels serve as windows into the cultures and histories of different periods, allowing readers to gain a broader perspective on the world.

4. Developing Emotional Intelligence and Empathy

One of the most powerful effects of reading novels is their ability to cultivate empathy and emotional intelligence. By immersing themselves in the lives of fictional characters, readers can explore a wide range of emotions and situations, helping them better understand the feelings of others in real life.

In *The Kite Runner* by Khaled Hosseini, readers experience the complexities of guilt, redemption, and the bonds of friendship and family through the eyes of Amir, a boy growing up in Afghanistan. The novel helps readers understand the emotional struggles of its characters, fostering a more profound sense of empathy for those who experience trauma, displacement, and guilt.

Studying novels allows students to vicariously experience complex emotions and social situations, making them more emotionally attuned and empathetic.

5. Encouraging Creativity and Imagination

Novels are works of imagination, and studying them encourages readers to tap into their creative potential. Whether it's the magical worlds of fantasy novels or the intricate plots of mysteries, novels inspire readers to think beyond the limits of reality and imagine new possibilities.

J.R.R. Tolkien's *The Lord of the Rings* immerses readers in an entirely different world filled with mythical creatures, languages, and landscapes. Through Tolkien's detailed world-building and imaginative storytelling, readers are encouraged to stretch their imaginations and envision worlds beyond their own.

Studying novels, particularly those in the science fiction and fantasy genres, fosters creativity and helps students think more flexibly and imaginatively, which are valuable skills in both personal and professional contexts.

6. Understanding Language and Style

The novel is a narrative form and a canvas for linguistic creativity. By studying novels, students appreciate the beauty of language and the various ways it can convey ideas, emotions, and atmospheres. Every novel has its style, and studying a range of novels allows readers to explore different narrative voices, tones, and structures.

In *Beloved* by Toni Morrison, language becomes an important storytelling tool. Morrison's lyrical prose and her use of non-linear narrative help to convey the haunting and traumatic legacy of slavery. By studying the novel, students learn how the author's stylistic choices contribute to the emotional and thematic power of the story.

By analysing the language and style of different novels, students develop a greater appreciation for literary artistry and a deeper understanding of how language can evoke emotions, ideas, and imagery.

7. Exploring Ethical and Moral Questions

Novels often confront readers with complex ethical dilemmas and moral questions, offering a space to explore and reflect on right and wrong, justice and injustice, and good and evil. Through the characters' experiences, readers can engage with these moral questions and develop their understanding of complex ethical issues.

In *The Road* by Cormac McCarthy, a father and son struggle to survive in a post-apocalyptic world. The novel raises questions about survival, morality, and the lengths a person will go to protect a loved one. Readers are prompted to consider what it means to maintain one's humanity in extreme circumstances.

By studying novels that explore ethical questions, students are encouraged to think deeply about their values and beliefs while also considering the perspectives of others.

8. Connecting to Universal Themes

Many novels explore universal themes—love, death, family, freedom, and the search for meaning—that resonate across cultures and periods. These themes speak to the core of human existence, and studying them helps readers connect with the more significant questions and concerns that define our shared humanity.

Gabriel García Márquez's *One Hundred Years of Solitude* explores themes of love, death, fate, and the cyclical nature of history through the lens of a single-family in the fictional town of Macondo. The novel's exploration of these universal themes has made it a timeless and influential work in world literature.

Students can see how literature reflects the human experience and connects individuals across time and space by studying novels that address universal themes.

Studying novels is more than just an academic exercise; it is a journey into the depths of human experience, culture, language, and emotion. Novels allow readers to reflect on their lives and world while providing a space for imagination, empathy, and moral reflection. By engaging with novels, students improve their critical thinking and analytical skills and better understand themselves and others. So why study novels? **Because they are windows into the human soul, we can better understand the world and our place within it through them.**

As we reach the end of this journey through the captivating world of novels, it's time to reflect on the key themes and insights we've explored together. Novels have travelled a long path from their humble beginnings in oral traditions to the multifaceted literary forms of today. Each era has added its unique flavour, cultivating an ever-evolving garden of stories that enrich our understanding of the human experience.

Throughout the chapters, we've delved into the intricacies of narrative structures, character development, and thematic complexity. From the straightforward tales of early storytelling to the fragmented narratives of postmodernism, novels have continuously pushed boundaries, offering readers new ways to engage with literature. By revisiting these key themes, we reinforce how richly layered and multidimensional novels can be, reflecting the complexities of life itself.

Our exploration doesn't end here. As you close this book, consider it the beginning of a lifelong adventure in reading and analysing literature. Countless novels await you, each with a universe of characters, settings, and ideas. Diversifying your reading across different genres can open up new worlds and perspectives. Whether you're drawn to Gothic fiction's eerie vibes or speculative literature's imaginative realms, each genre holds unique treasures. Don't limit yourself to what feels safe or familiar; let curiosity guide you, and you'll find that every novel, no matter how different, has something valuable to offer.

Engaging with peers can also deepen your appreciation and understanding of literature. Participate in book clubs, join online forums, or discuss books with friends and classmates. These discussions can provide fresh perspectives and insights that you might not have considered on your own. Engaging with others allows you to see different angles of a story, enhancing your analytical skills and enriching your reading experience.

Armed with the tools of literary analysis discussed in this guide, you are now equipped to approach novels with a critical eye. Analysing literature is akin to peeling back layers of an onion; with each layer removed, new meanings and interpretations emerge. When encountering a novel, ask yourself probing questions: What are the underlying themes? How do the characters evolve? What narrative techniques does the author use to convey deeper meanings? Employ various lenses—feminist, Marxist, psychoanalytic, or any other critical framework—to dissect the text and uncover hidden nuances. Critical thinking involves finding faults and engaging deeply with the material to appreciate its richness.

Furthermore, don't shy away from challenging work. Some novels may seem daunting at first glance, but with patience and perseverance, they often reveal themselves to be profoundly rewarding. Complex texts push you to think harder and dig deeper, sharpening your analytical abilities and broadening your intellectual horizons. Remember, every complex novel was written with intention and purpose; your task as a reader is to unravel those intentions and understand the broader societal and cultural contexts in which the work exists.

Novels hold a special place in society, acting as mirrors and windows. They reflect societal norms, values, and conflicts while offering glimpses into lives and experiences far removed from our own. We can explore different cultures, historical periods, and social issues through literature, gaining insights that foster empathy and understanding. In a world that often feels divided, novels remind us of our shared humanity, bridging gaps between diverse perspectives and experiences.

As you continue your literary journey, consider the broader role of novels in shaping culture and society. Literature can provoke thought, challenge established norms, and inspire change. Great stories often catalyse social movements, sparking conversations about justice, equality, and human rights. Engaging with these works critically and thoughtfully makes you part of a more extensive dialogue transcending any book's pages.

> *"Reading novels also encourages personal growth by providing opportunities for introspection and self-reflection. Characters' struggles and triumphs can mirror our own, offering comfort and guidance in times of need. The stories we read shape our thoughts, beliefs, and actions, influencing how we perceive and interact with the world. In recognising the transformative power of literature, we embrace its potential to change our minds and hearts."*

In conclusion, this book has aimed to equip you with the knowledge and tools necessary to delve deeper into the world of novels and literary analysis. Whether you are a student seeking to enhance your comprehension and appreciation of literature, an educator looking for practical teaching strategies, or a curious young adult eager to explore new literary horizons, I hope this guide has provided valuable insights and inspiration.

Remember, the journey of literary exploration is never-ending. Each novel is an invitation to uncover new depths of meaning, challenge your preconceptions, and expand your understanding of the world. So, keep reading, analysing, and discussing. Let your love for literature propel you forward, and may every novel you encounter enrich your mind and soul.